THE BIKE BOOK

LIFESTYLE. PASSION. DESIGN.

teNeues

TABLE OF CONTENTS

SPORT BIKES

URBAN BIKES

UTILITY BIKES

E-BIKES

ACCESSORIES

SPECIAL & CONCEPT BIKES

CREATIVE BIKE STORAGE

PHOTO CREDITS & IMPRINT

LIFESTYLE. PASSION. DESIGN.

The feeling of freedom experienced on a bike is like nothing else in the world. With that first liberating ride—the first excursion on two wheels—comes a boundless joy that is never to be forgotten. Only a bike combines emotion and reason in such a unique way. It's the most efficient and ecofriendly means of human locomotion. No other invention can cover more distance per unit of energy consumed.

But today, bikes are much more than simple means of transportation or load-carrying devices. Bikes are cool, they're "in," they're lifestyle objects. Design, look, hightech, and luxury are just as important as the passion of designers, frame builders, and users. A plain, understated urban bike can be every bit as fascinating as a carbon-fiber time-trial bike built for minimum wind resistance using supercomputers. Classic bikes from Britain, France, and Italy have inspired a retro trend, with fan clubs rhapsodizing and blogging about single speeds and fixies. The e-bike category covers an unbelievable range, from the perfect city and cargo bikes to high-powered Monster scooters. Mountain bikes have brought new technologies to the biking world, including spring suspensions and disc brakes. Designers and artists are continually giving the 100-year-old bike concept a fresh new look, refining their models into showpieces by means of valuable accoutrements like gold and diamonds, or exotic materials like snakeskin leather.

The pages of this elaborately styled book contain the world's most unusual, most expensive, most innovative, and trendiest bikes—as portrayed by modern photographers, often from surprising new angles. This volume brings together a collection of visual and technical masterpieces by bike builders from around the world, milestones in bike design to awaken the readers' deepest longings—to jump on a bike and re-experience the freedom that only a bike can give; to cruise carefree through the city, traverse entire continents, cross the Alps under their own steam, sail down country roads in the most beautiful regions of the world—or just park the bike in their apartment and admire the clear lines, flawless craftsmanship, and choice materials. In other words, to enjoy everything a state-of-the-art bike has to offer today: lifestyle, passion, design.

Das Gefühl der Freiheit, das man auf einem Fahrrad empfindet, ist unvergleichlich. Die erste losgelöste Fahrt, den ersten Ausflug auf zwei Rädern, das grenzenlose Glücksgefühl dabei vergisst man nie. Nur ein Fahrrad verbindet auf einmalige Weise Emotionen und Vernunft. Es ist das effizienteste und umweltfreundlichste Fortbewegungsmittel des Menschen. Mit keiner anderen Erfindung schafft man es, eine größere Strecke pro verbrauchter Energieeinheit zurückzulegen.

Doch ist ein Fahrrad inzwischen weit mehr als ein Transportmittel oder schlichter Lastenträger. Fahrräder sind cool, Fahrräder sind in, Fahrräder sind Lifestyle-Objekte. Design, Optik, Hightech und Luxus spielen eine ebenso große Rolle wie die Leidenschaft der Konstrukteure, Rahmenbauer und der Nutzer. Ein schlichtes, auf Understatement gestyltes Urban Bike kann hierbei für ebenso viel Faszination sorgen wie eine Zeitfahrmaschine aus Carbonfasern, die mit Supercomputern für minimalen Luftwiderstand gebaut wurde. Klassische Räder aus Großbritannien, Frankreich und Italien haben eine Retro-Welle ausgelöst, Fangemeinden schwärmen und bloggen über Singlespeeder und Fixies. Die Kategorie E-Bikes bewegt sich in einem unglaublichen Spektrum, vom perfekten City- und Lastenrad bis zum wattstarken Monster-Mobil. Mountainbikes haben neue Technologien wie gefederte Fahrwerke und Scheibenbremsen in die Radwelt gebracht. Designer und Künstler geben dem über 100 Jahre alten Thema Fahrrad immer wieder einen neuen, frischen Look, veredeln Modelle zu Show-Objekten mit wertvollen Applikationen wie Gold und Diamanten oder exotischen Materialien wie Schlangenleder.

Die ungewöhnlichsten, teuersten, innovativsten und trendigsten Räder werden in diesem aufwendig gestalteten Buch präsentiert. In Szene gesetzt von modernen Fotografen, oft aus überraschend neuen Blickwinkeln. Dieser Band versammelt die visuellen und technischen Meisterstücke von Fahrradbauern rund um den Globus, die Meilensteine im Bike-Design, die die Lust beim Betrachter fördern: Die Lust, sich aufs Rad zu setzen und sich daran zu erinnern, welche Freiheiten ein Rad beschert. Sorglos durch die Stadt zu cruisen, ganze Kontinente zu bereisen, die Alpen aus eigener Kraft zu überqueren, über die Landstraßen der schönsten Regionen zu fliegen. Oder es einfach in die Wohnung zu stellen und sich an den klaren Linien, der makellosen Verarbeitung und den ausgesuchten Materialien zu erfreuen. Zu genießen, was ein modernes Fahrrad heute ausmacht: Lifestyle, Passion, Design.

Impossible de comparer la sensation de liberté que procure la pratique du vélo. Difficile d'oublier les moments d'intense bonheur qu'ont été la première fois sans les petites roues ou la première vraie promenade. Union unique d'émotions et de bon sens, la bicyclette est le moyen de transport le plus efficace et le plus respectueux de l'environnement jamais inventé. Nul autre ne permet d'effectuer un aussi long trajet pour la même consommation d'énergie.

Le vélo ne se cantonne plus à son simple rôle de véhicule personnel ou utilitaire. Cool et tendance, il est un véritable objet-symbole du style de vie de son propriétaire. Design, look, technologie et luxe comptent aujourd'hui tout autant que la passion du constructeur, le choix du cadre ou l'utilisation prévue. Dès lors, un vélo urbain axé sur le style peut susciter autant de fascination qu'une machine de contre-la-montre en carbone conçue pour offrir le meilleur aérodynamisme, comme en témoigne la vague rétro née en Grande-Bretagne, en France et en Italie, venue frapper les bicyclettes classiques, ou le mouvement Fixies qui inspire de nombreux bloggeurs et rassemble, autour des mono-vitesses, de véritables communautés de fans enthousiastes. Sur le plan technologique, les vélos électriques et leur gamme incroyablement vaste, qui va du vélo cargo idéal en zone urbaine aux monstres de rapidité dopés aux watts, suivent la voie ouverte par les VTT, qui ont introduit des innovations comme les fourches et les bras oscillants suspendus, mais aussi les freins à disque. Par ailleurs, des designers et des artistes rafraichissent l'image de la petite reine désormais centenaire en élevant certains modèles au rang d'objets d'exposition, une fois parés d'or, de diamants, ou de matériaux exotiques comme du cuir de serpent.

Le présent ouvrage est le fruit de la recherche des vélos les plus extraordinaires, les plus chers, les plus innovants et les plus en vogue, magnifiquement mis en scène par des photographes en vue, souvent sous un angle aussi novateur qu'étonnant. Ce volume réunit les chefs-d'œuvre de fabricants de cycles du monde entier qui posent de nouveaux jalons pour le secteur en termes esthétiques et techniques, mais aussi suscitent l'envie du lecteur... l'envie de rouler à deux roues et de retrouver le souvenir de cette liberté qu'offre le vélo, de se promener nonchalamment dans la ville, d'aller à la découverte de continents, de traverser les Alpes à la force des pédales, de parcourir les routes des plus belles régions ou simplement d'exposer son bijou chez soi, de se délecter de ses lignes claires, de sa conception impeccable et de ses matériaux soigneusement sélectionnés. Ce sont là autant d'occasions de profiter pleinement de ce qu'offre une bicyclette de nos jours: lifestyle, passion, design.

Thomas Rögner

SPORT BIKES

FOR THE MODEST POSER

TRAVELISSIMO, HAMPSTEN CYCLES

In 1988, Andy Hampsten flew up the Gavia Pass to become the first and, so far, the only American to achieve an overall victory in the Giro d'Italia. His love of Italy is expressed in the classic frame constructed of Columbus steel tubing. Thanks to S&S Machine Works couplers, this racing bike with a '60s look is easy to disassemble and transport. The classic center-pull brakes and wider tires are ideal for the Strade Bianche, the legendary white roads of Tuscany. Travelissimo is a touring racer that's loaded with character and charisma.

1988 flog Andy Hampsten den Gaviapass hinauf und sicherte sich, als erster und einziger Amerikaner bis dato, den Gesamtsieg des Giro d'Italia. Seine Liebe zu Italien manifestiert sich in diesem klassischen Rahmen aus Columbus-Stahlrohren. Der Renner im Look der 60er Jahre ist durch die S-&-S-Machineworks-Steckverbindungen problemlos zu zerlegen und zu transportieren. Die klassischen Mittelzugbremsen und die breiteren Reifen sind ideal für die legendären weißen Straßen der Toskana, die Strade Bianche. Ein Reise-Renner mit Charakter und Ausstrahlung.

En 1988, en dominant la montée du col de Gavia, Andy Hampsten s'assurait la victoire générale du Giro. À ce jour, il est le seul américain à l'avoir remporté. Son amour pour l'Italie se retrouve dans ce cadre classique en tube d'acier Columbus. Le vélo de course reprend une esthétique résolument années 60 ainsi qu'un système S&S Machineworks pour démonter facilement le cadre et faciliter le transport. Les freins à tirage central et les pneus larges sont parfaits pour les légendaires routes blanches de la Toscane: les Strade Bianche. Un vélo de course qui ne manque ni de caractère, ni de style.

Country: USA · Year: 2010 · Weight: 9 kg · Frame: Columbus Spirit steel · Gears: 20 · Tyres: 700cx 33mm / 27" · Brakes: Center-pull

TRAVEL IN STYLE

ARTISAN LUGGED TRAVEL TANDEM, BILENKY CYCLE WORKS

Clearly, there can be no comparison between creations by Stephen Bilenky, who has been building steel frames for over 30 years, and bikes "off the rack." His crew at Bilenky Cycle Works in Philadelphia shares his same philosophy and builds stylish and unusual bikes—like the Travel Tandem, which can be fully disassembled and whose retro look makes it perfect for touring Provence or Tuscany. The S & S couplings provide stable connections, and the two traveling cases included with the bike ensures safe transport on a flight to Europe.

Wenn jemand wie Stephen Bilenky seit über 30 Jahren Stahlrahmen herstellt, ist klar, dass man seine Kreationen nicht mit Rädern von der Stange vergleichen kann. Seine Crew von Bilenky Cycle Works in Philadelphia denkt und arbeitet ebenso philosophisch wie er und baut stylische, ungewöhnliche Räder wie das zerlegbare Travel Tandem, das durch seinen Retro-Look wie geschaffen ist für Touren durch die Provence oder die Toskana. Die S-&-S-Kupplungen sorgen für eine stabile Verbindung, die zwei mitgelieferten Reisekoffer für einen sicheren Transport beim Flug nach Europa.

Il est impossible de comparer avec le reste du marché les créations de quelqu'un comme Stephen Bilenky qui crée des cadres en acier depuis 30 ans. Son équipe de Bilenky Cycle Works, installée à Philadelphie, pense et travaille avec les mêmes principes, le même style, pour réaliser des vélos hors du commun comme ce Travel Tandem, dont le look rétro conviendra parfaitement aux randonnées à travers la Provence ou la Toscane. Pour un transfert en toute sécurité, il est livré avec deux valises de transport. Bien que démontable, le cadre montre une parfaite stabilité grâce aux raccords S & S.

Country: USA · Year: 2010 · Weight: 21 kg · Frame: Reynolds 531 and Columbus Zona · Gears: 27 · Tyres: 28 x 1.25" · Brakes: Cantilever

STEEL IS KING

CIELO SPORTIF RACER SE, CHRIS KING

A wonderfully distinctive steel frame from Cielo, a bike brand built by the renowned component company Chris King. The KVA MS2 Stainless Steel tubeset is flawlessly and durably crafted by this Oregon parts specialist to the same standards as their legendary headsets, hubs and bottom brackets. The welds are a dream come true—the Cielo frame is TIG-welded in Portland. With details like the computer-machined fork, monogrammed dropouts and seat stay plugs, and integrated seat clamps, this steel frame goes far beyond simple craftsmanship. "Steel is more than real" when it's a Cielo by Chris King.

Ein wunderschöner klarer Stahlrahmen von der Firma der Komponentenspezialisten Chris King. Die KVA MS2-Rohre und sind so makellos und langlebig verarbeitet wie die legendären Steuersätze und Naben der Teilefirma aus Oregon. Die Schweißnähte sind ein Traum, der Cielo-Rahmen wird TIG-geschweißt in Portland. Details wie die computergefräste Gabel, Monogramme auf den Ausfallenden und die integrierte Sattelstützenklemmung heben den Stahlrahmen über profanes Handwerk hinaus. „Steel is more than real" bei Cielo.

La société de Chris King, roi du composant, signe ici un magnifique cadre en acier aux lignes claires. L'usinage soigné et résistant des tubes KVA MS2 sont à la hauteur des légendaires jeux de direction et des moyeux du fabricant de l'Oregon. Le merveilleux travail de soudure sur le cadre Cielo est réalisé à Portland selon le procédé TIG. Certains détails, comme le fraisage de la fourche assisté par ordinateur, le monogramme des pattes et le collier de tige de selle intégré, élèvent ce cadre en acier au rang de véritable bijou profane. «Steel is more than real» par Cielo.

Country: USA · Year: 2011 · Weight: 8.16 kg · Frame: Stainless steel · Gears: 22 · Tyres: 28C
Brakes: Campagnolo Dual Pivot Road Caliper

SUPERLIGHT

CERVÉLO R5CA, CERVÉLO

The weight of this Cervélo frame is too good to be true. With its understated matte finish, the R5ca frame weighs less than 700 grams, as well as being extremely rigid. For this purpose-built model, the Canadian company's specially founded Project California research department applied the latest bottom bracket standards, such as BBright, to turn every watt of the rider's energy into forward propulsion. The special matte paint adds no purely cosmetic grams to the weight and, in combination with shiny highlights, creates a restrained visual effect that doesn't detract from this racing machine's potential.

Traumgewicht für den Rahmen dieses Cervélo: Unter 700 Gramm liegt der in mattem Understatement gehaltene Rahmen des R5ca und ist dabei extrem steif. Die eigens gegründete Forschungsabteilung Project California der kanadischen Firma nutzt bei diesem auf Funktion ausgerichteten Modell neueste Tretlager-Standards wie BBright, um jedes Watt des Fahrers in Vortrieb umzusetzen. Der matte Speziallack spart kosmetische Gramm ein und ergibt mit dem glänzenden Dekor eine zurückhaltende Optik, die nicht vom Potenzial dieser Rennmaschine ablenkt.

Un poids de rêve pour le cadre de ce Cervélo: pesant moins de 700 grammes, le cadre du R5ca d'une simple finition mate, offre une extrême rigidité. Project California, le département de recherche de la société canadienne Cervélo, a équipé ce modèle résolument orienté performance du tout dernier pédalier BBright afin de restituer toute la puissance de l'utilisateur au watt près. La peinture mate spéciale témoigne de la chasse au superflu et produit, au milieu des couleurs bariolées de la concurrence, un effet sobre qui laisse la vedette au potentiel de cette bête de course.

Country: Canada · Year: 2012 · Weight: Under 0.7 kg · Frame: Carbon

NATURAL VELOCITY

BAMBOO PRO / DRAGONFLY PRO, CALFEE DESIGN

To achieve the maximum stiffness-to-weight (STW) ratio, Calfee integrates additional boron fibers into the Dragonfly's frame. The tubes and lugs are made of high modulus carbon. For the bamboo, the California company calls on its fiber expertise to create a racing bike made of natural materials that is suitable for competitive use. Over 40 hours of processing are required to produce the bamboo frame, whose supple riding characteristics even exceed those of carbon and titanium frames, and whose ecological footprint is also far superior.

Um das maximale Steifigkeits-Gewichts-Verhältnis, genannt STW, zu erzielen, integriert Calfee zusätzlich Boronfasern in den Rahmen des Dragonfly. Die Rohre und Muffen werden aus High-Modulus-Carbon gefertigt. Beim Bamboo setzt die kalifornische Firma ihr Know-how im Faserbereich um in ein wettbewerbstaugliches Rennrad aus dem Naturbaustoff. Über 40 Arbeitsstunden stecken im Bamboo-Rahmen, dessen geschmeidige Fahreigenschaften sogar die von Carbon- oder Titanrahmen übertreffen sollen. Und die Öko-Bilanz fällt ungleich besser aus für diesen Bambusrahmen.

Pour obtenir un rapport poids/rigidité maximal, aussi appelé STW, Calfee intègre des fibres de bore dans le cadre du Dragonfly. Les tubes et manchons sont réalisés en carbone à haut module. Dans le cas du Bamboo, la société californienne met tout son savoir-faire en matière de fibres dans un vélo de course en matériau naturel apte à la compétition. Pas moins de 40 heures de travail sont nécessaires pour conférer au cadre en bambou une souplesse d'utilisation supérieure à celle des cadres en carbone ou en titane, également surclassés sur le plan du bilan écologique.

Country: USA · Year: 2005/2001 · Weight: 7.25 kg / 6.35 kg · Frame: Smoked and heat treated bamboo with hemp fiber lugs and plant based high performance eco resin / High modulus carbon w/boron fiber and plant based high performance eco resin · Gears: 20 Tyres: 700C · Brakes: Rim brake

SPEED MACHINE

PLASMA PREMIUM, SCOTT

Developed as a professional time trial bike, the Scott Plasma Premium can give any triathlete the edge in a battle against the wind. Codeveloper Simon Smart applied knowledge of aerodynamics that he gained working for a Formula One racing team. Visual highlights of this 7.5-kilogram time trial machine are the contoured head tube with integrated fork and the surface-dynamic seat tube. And, of course, the SRAM Red and wheels from Zipp aero specialists are equal to the most extreme challenges.

Als Profirad fürs Zeitfahren entwickelt, kann das Scott Plasma Premium jedem Triathleten einen Vorteil im Kampf gegen den Wind verschaffen. Der Mitentwickler Simon Smart arbeitete für einen Formel-1-Rennstall und brachte sein Wissen in Sachen Aerodynamik ein. Optische Leckerbissen an der 7,5-Kilo-Zeitfahrmaschine sind das profilierte Steuerrohr mit integrierter Gabel und die flächig-dynamische Sitzrohrlösung. Dass die Ausstattung mit der Red von SRAM und Laufrädern des Aero-Spezialisten Zipp ebenfalls höchsten Ansprüchen genügt, versteht sich von selbst.

Développé comme un vélo professionnel de contre-la-montre, le Scott Plasma Premium procure au triathlonien un avantage conséquent en matière de résistance au vent. Simon Smart, qui a participé à sa conception, a apporté ses connaissances en aérodynamisme acquises en Formule 1. Avec sa douille de direction profilée, directement dans le prolongement de la fourche, et son système de tige de selle plate, cette monture de contre-la-montre est un vrai bijou. Bien sûr, l'équipement est à la hauteur de ses ambitions avec un groupe SRAM Red et des roues conçues par le spécialiste de l'aéronautique Zipp.

Country: Switzerland · Year: 2012 · Weight: 7.5 kg · Frame: HMX-NET Carbon · Gears: SRAM Red Carbon ceramic, 2 x 10
Tyres: 28" · Brakes: SRAM Red black, Zipp carbon pads (front); Shimano 7900, Zipp carbon pads (rear)

ITALIAN LEGEND

PRO ESTRADA, CINELLI

Legendary handlebars, stems, and lugs that are used by almost every Italian bicycle manufacturer—that's Cinelli's calling card. The first Cinelli frame, the Super Corsa, was ridden by Fausto Coppi. The iconic company founded by racer Cino Cinelli in the late 1940's has carried its traditional values into the present. Now under the ownership of Columbus-owner Antonio Colombo, the company's top model, the Pro Estrada, exemplifies the optimal processing of carbon fibers and state-of-the-art frame design.

Legendäre Lenker, Vorbauten und Muffen, die fast jeder italienische Radhersteller verwendete, sind die Aushängeschilder von Cinelli. Fausto Coppi fuhr einen der ersten Cinelli-Rahmen, das Super Corsa. Die Ende der 40er Jahre von Rennfahrer Cino Cinelli gegründete Kultfirma hat ihre traditionellen Werte in die Gegenwart transportiert. Nun im Besitz von Columbus-Eigner Antonio Colombo, werden im Spitzenmodell Pro Estrada optimale Verarbeitung von Carbonfasern und modernstes Rahmendesign verwirklicht.

Des cintres, des potences et des manchons légendaires, qui étaient utilisés jadis par presque tous les fabricants italiens, ont fait la renommée de Cinelli. Fausto Coppi roulait avec l'un des premiers cadres Cinelli: le Super Corsa. L'entreprise culte fondée à la fin des années 40 par le coureur Cino Cinelli a porté ses valeurs traditionnelles jusqu'à nos jours. Aujourd'hui dirigée par Antonio Colombo, propriétaire de Colombus, la Société produit le Pro Estrada, modèle phare de la marque, réalisé en fibres de carbone, sur la base d'un cadre au design des plus modernes.

Country: Italy · Year: 2007 · Weight: 860 g (frame); 380 g (fork) · Frame: Carbon fiber · Gears: Campagnolo Super Record 2 x 11 Tyres: 28" · Brakes: Campagnolo Super Record Carbon Caliper

CELESTIAL QUEEN
OLTRE SUPER RECORD 11, BIANCHI

Molto italiano. The name Bianchi is associated with cycling legends like Coppi, Gimondi and Pantani. The Oltre here in the classic version, is one of the most advanced bikes ever made by this traditional Bergamo company. Carbon strips are molded into the carbon structure of the head tube for extreme stiffness and torsional rigidity. At the same time, ultra-thin seat stays ensure high comfort for a racing bike in its performance class. Aerodynamic features from the Crono time trial bike ensure an aero shape and elegant design. Nothing fits Oltre better than Campagnolo´s top-of-the-line Super Record 11.

Molto italiano. Mit Bianchi verbindet man Radsportlegenden wie Coppi, Gimondi, Pantani. Das Oltre, hier im klassischen Celeste, ist eines der faszinierendsten Räder der Traditionsfirma aus Bergamo. Die Hochmodul-Carbonfasern im Steuerkopfbereich erzeugen extreme Steifigkeit. Gleichzeitig sorgen ultradünne Sitzstreben für ungewohnt hohen Komfort an einem Rennrad dieser Leistungsklasse. Eleganz und Geschwindigkeitsvorteile bringen die aerodynamischen Anleihen vom Zeitfahrrad Crono. Nichts könnte ans Oltre besser passen als die Campa-Spitzengruppe Super Record 11.

Molto italiano. Bianchi est directement associée aux légendes de la petite reine comme Coppi, Gimondi, Pantani. L'Oltre, ici dans sa version classique Celeste, est l'un des vélos les plus fascinants de l'institution de Bergame. La fibre de carbone haut module utilisée pour la douille de direction est le gage d'une extrême rigidité. Par ailleurs, si les haubans ultrafins offrent un confort exceptionnel pour un vélo de course de ce niveau, les emprunts au vélo de contre-la-montre Crono lui confèrent élégance et aérodynamisme. Question groupe, que rêver de mieux que l'exceptionnel Campagnolo Super Record 11.

Country: Italy · Year: 2011 · Weight: 6.7 kg · Frame: Oltre Carbon · Gears: 22 · Tyres: 28" · Brakes: Campagnolo Super Record

LIMITED EDITION

NIGHTSTREAM, VANDEYK CONTEMPORARY CYCLES

Limited edition works of art. For each of its series, VANDEYK issues only 25 bikes. Models by former racer Arendt van Deyk meet the highest standards in terms of materials, design and construction. Artist Harry Seifert designed the Nightstream with its hand-built Columbus XCr frame and fully integrated Shimano Dura-Ace Di2 groupset. Bikes are painted by a company specializing in highly exclusive supersport cars. Each color is applied in a single layer on a white base, finishing with the main color of matte black.

Limitierte Kunst: Nur 25 Exemplare werden pro Serie einer VANDEYK-Produktion aufgelegt. Höchste Ansprüche an Material, Gestaltung und Ausführung zeichnen die Modelle des ehemaligen Rennfahrers Arendt van Deyk aus. Künstler Harry Seifert gestaltete das Design des Nightstream: handgearbeiteter Columbus-XCr-Rahmen mit vollintegrierter Shimano Dura-Ace Di2-Schaltung. Die Lackierung erfolgt durch eine Firma, spezialisiert auf hochexklusive Supersport Cars. Jede Farbe wird in einer singulären Schicht auf weißem Grund aufgetragen, die mattschwarze Hauptfarbe steht am Ende des Prozesses.

Œuvres d'art: VANDEYK ne produit que 25 exemplaires par série. Les modèles de l'ancien coureur Arendt van Deyk se caractérisent par un niveau d'exigence maximal en termes de matériau, d'équipement et de finition. Le design du Nightstream est l'œuvre de l'artiste Harry Seifert: le cadre Columbus XCr a été travaillé à la main et comporte un groupe Shimano Dura-Ace Di2. La peinture est réalisée par une société spécialisée dans les voitures de sport les plus sélect. Curieusement, chaque couleur est appliquée en simple couche sur une base blanche, la couleur principale noir-mat ne venant qu'en fin de processus.

Country: Germany · Year: 2011 · Weight: 7.5 kg · Frame: Columbus XCr Stainless Steel Gears: Shimano Dura-Ace Di2, 2 x 10 · Tyres: 28" · Brakes: Shimano Dura-Ace

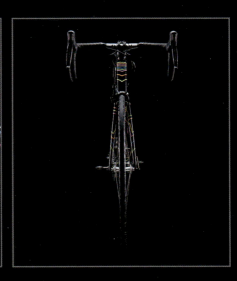

BMW GOES BICYCLE

M-BIKE CARBON RACER, BMW

At BMW, the M Series stands for "motorsports" and a consistent philosophy of lightweight construction. When it comes to BMW racing bikes, M represents extreme athleticism with a record low weight. At a mere 16.31 pounds, the Munich auto manufacturer's Carbon Racer barely tips the scale. Rims, seat inlay, and handlebar grips are all M-design red and provide a nice contrast to the frame's anthracite carbon look, as does the striking M logo on the top tube.

Die M-Serie steht bei BMW für den Motorsportsektor und konsequente Leichtbau-Philosophie. Beim BMW-Rennrad signalisiert das M höchste Sportlichkeit mit einem Rekordgewicht. Bei lediglich 7400 Gramm bleibt die Skala beim Carbon Racer der Münchner Autobauer stehen. Felgen, Sattelinlay und Griffband sind im M-Design-Rot gestaltet und bilden einen gelungenen Kontrast zur anthrazitfarbenen Carbon-Optik des Rahmens, ebenso wie das markante M-Logo auf dem Oberrohr.

Chez BMW, la série M indique l'intervention du département Motorsport et donc l'utilisation de matériaux légers. Sur un vélo de course, le M se traduit par une orientation sport radicale et un poids record. Le Carbon Racer de la firme de Munich n'affiche pas plus de 7.4 kg sur la balance. Les jantes, la pointe de la selle et le grip arborent le rouge caractéristique d'une conception M et contrastent joliment avec l'aspect anthracite du carbone du cadre estampillé d'un M sur la barre horizontale.

Country: Germany · Year: 2011/12 · Weight: 7.4 kg · Frame: Carbon (high modulus) · Gears: Shimano Ultegra 20 speed · Tyres: 28" Brakes: Shimano Ultegra

RIDERS ON THE STORM

AERO 2, STORCK

With its flat frame elements and seamless component integration, Storck's Aero 2 is practically immune to wind resistance. The stem and top tube form a straight line, the Scapula fork fits beautifully with the frame, and the caliper brakes are an integral part of the frame. The Aero 2's design is compatible with the Shimano Dura-Ace Di2 electronic groupset. The battery casing is aerodynamically positioned behind the Aero seat post. The tricolor paintwork emphasizes the dynamic character of this ultimate time trial machine.

Flächige Rahmenformen und nahtlose Integration der Komponenten lassen dem Luftwiderstand an Storcks Aero 2 keine Chance. Der Vorbau liegt in einer Linie mit dem Oberrohr, die Scapula-Gabel und der Rahmen gehen eine formschöne Verbindung ein, die Felgenbremsen sind integrativer Teil des Rahmens. Das Aero 2 ist konsequent auf Shimanos elektronische Schaltung Dura-Ace Di2 ausgelegt, das Batteriegehäuse liegt strömungs- günstig hinter der Aero-Sattelstütze. Die dreifarbige Lackierung unterstreicht den aggressiven Charakter dieser konsequenten Zeitmaschine.

Les formes profilées du cadre et l'intégration parfaite des composants permettent à l'Aero 2 de Storck de se jouer du vent. La potence est exactement dans le prolongement de la barre horizontale, tandis que la fourche Scapula est alignée sur la douille de direction et que les freins sur jante font partie intégrante du cadre. L'Aero 2 est équipé du groupe électronique Shimano Dura-Ace Di2, dont la batterie, idéalement placée derrière la tige de selle, n'offre aucune prise au vent. La peinture tricolore souligne le caractère agressif de cette redoutable mécanique de contre-la-montre.

Country: Germany · Year: 2009 · Weight: 2.59 kg (frameset) · Frame: Carbon · Gears: For all electronic shift systems
Tyres: 28" · Brakes: Integrated carbon brakes

SWISS PRECISION
GOOMAH MEETS LIGHTWEIGHT, GOOMAH / LIGHTWEIGHT

When the Swiss company Assos combines state-of-the-art know-how with its own roots and transfers this knowledge to a new company the results are spectacular. As early as 1976, Assos was building a carbon frame that was way ahead of its time. In the case of the Goomah G.731, this means using three different strengths of high modulus carbon fiber. The Assos Centro Studio, which is Assos' R&D department in the Swiss canton of Ticino, developed the limited-edition Goomah frame with and for the équipeEXPLOIT. Goomah is now a new company and brand. The German lightweight racing wheels perfect this precision machine.

Wenn die Schweizer Firma Assos aktuelles Know-how mit ihren Wurzeln verbindet und dieses Wissen in eine neue Firma transferiert, entsteht etwas Spektakuläres. Bereits 1976 baute Assos einen Carbonrahmen, der seiner Zeit weit voraus war. Der in limitierter Stückzahl angebotene Goomah-Rahmen wurde ursprünglich vom Assos Centro Studio, der Forschungs- und Entwicklungsabteilung im schweizerischen Tessin, mit der und für die équipeEXPLOIT entwickelt. Goomah ist nun eine eigene Firma und Marke. Beim Goomah G.731 wurden High-Modulus-Carbonfasern in drei unterschiedlichen Stärken verarbeitet. Die deutschen Lightweight-Laufräder vervollkommnen diese Präzisionsmaschine.

Lorsque l'entreprise suisse Assos renoue avec ses racines tout en plaçant son savoir-faire actuel dans une nouvelle société, le résultat est spectaculaire. Déjà en 1976, Assos construisait un cadre en carbone en avance sur son temps. Le cadre Goomah, de série limitée, a été développé initialement pour l'équipeEXPLOIT par Assos Centro Studio, le département de recherche et développement installé dans le canton du Tessin en Suisse. Goomah est désormais une société et une marque indépendante. Pour le Goomah G.731, la fibre de carbone haut module a été travaillée en trois différents niveaux de résistance. Les roues allemandes Lightweight apportent la touche finale à cette machine redoutable de précision.

Country: Switzerland · Year: 2011 · Weight: 6.1 kg (size L) · Frame: Carbon
Brakes: KCNC brakes, Swissstop Brake Pads

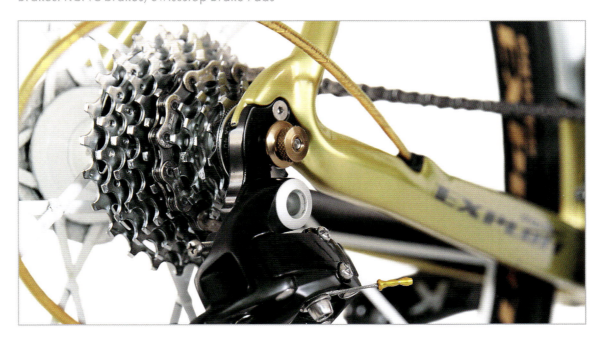

FRENCH CUISINE

TIME RXRS ULTEAM, TIME

Unlike almost every other bike manufacturer in the world, Time builds the RXR frame in its own production plants in France. Details like the tri-ovalized down tube, the aerodynamic features of the main frame, and the rear wheel integrated into the seat tube are what make the RXR unique. High modulus carbon with liquid crystal polyamide and aramid fiber inserts reduces vibration without negatively affecting stiffness. The RXR Ulteam is a professional racing machine designed for maximum performance in both windy and mountainous conditions.

Als einer der wenigen Hersteller weltweit fertigt Time den Rahmen des RXR in eigenen Produktionsstätten in Frankreich. Details wie das dreifach ovalisierte Unterrohr, die aerodynamischen Features am Hauptrahmen oder das ins Sitzrohr integrierte Hinterrad machen das RXR einmalig. Das High-Modulus-Carbonmaterial reduziert durch Inserts mit Polyamid-Flüssigkeitskristallen und Aramid-Fasern Vibrationen, ohne die Rahmensteifigkeit negativ zu beeinflussen. Eine Profi-Rennmaschine, die für maximale Leistung sowohl im Wind als auch am Berg ausgelegt ist.

Contrairement à la plupart des fabricants de cycles, Time produit le cadre du RXR dans ses propres ateliers en France. Le souci du détail, qui se retrouve dans le profil ovale du tube oblique, dans les éléments aérodynamiques sur le cadre ou dans le tube de selle qui épouse la courbe de la roue arrière, fait de ce RXR un vélo unique. Le carbone à haut module réduit les vibrations par l'incorporation de fibres polyamide à cristaux liquides et de fibres aramide, sans nuire à la rigidité du cadre. Cette machine de coureur professionnel a été conçue pour offrir les meilleures performances aussi bien dans les côtes que sur les routes exposées au vent.

Country: France · Year: 2011 · Weight: 6.9 kg · Frame: Carbon RTM technology
Gears: SRAM Red 2 x 10 · Tyres: 700 x 23C · Brakes: SRAM Red

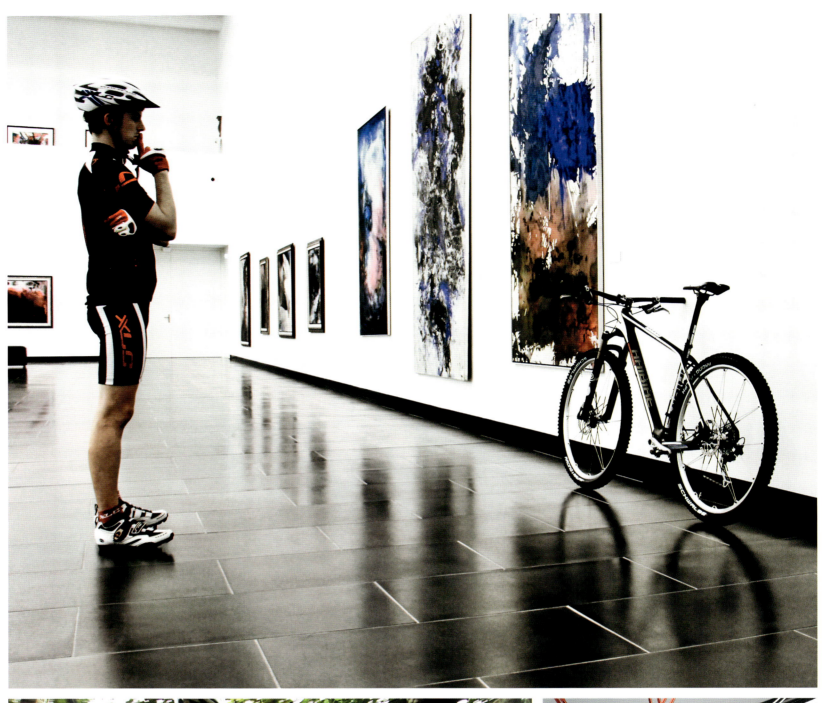

A REAL PIECE OF ART

GREED 29 RC, HAIBIKE

A 29-inch competitive marathon bike whose weight is under the magic 10-kilogram limit. The stylish Greed 29 RC earned the German company Haibike a coveted Eurobike Gold Award for outstanding innovation and design quality. The Greed also came out on top in tests conducted by trade magazines. Its most impressive feature is the high-modulus carbon frame built using Advanced Multiforming Technology and weighing a mere 1030 grams.

Ein wettbewerbstaugliches Marathonbike mit 29-Zöllern unter der magischen 10-Kilo-Grenze. Die deutsche Firma Haibike holte sich mit dem stylischen Greed 29 RC einen der begehrten Eurobike-Gold-Awards für herausragende Innovations- und Designqualität. Auch bei Tests von Fachmagazinen landet das Greed ganz vorne. Highlight ist der Rahmen aus High Modulus Carbon, verarbeitet in Advanced Multiforming Technology, der lediglich 1030 Gramm auf die Waage bringt.

Un vélo de cross-country de 29 pouces, fait pour la compétition, d'un poids inférieur au seuil magique des 10 kg. Avec ce magnifique Greed 29 RC, la société allemande Haibike a reçu le prix Eurobike du design et de l'innovation. À en juger les résultats des tests des magazines spécialisés qui le placent au premier rang, cette récompense ne doit rien au hasard. Il se caractérise notamment par un cadre en carbone haut module qui, réalisé à l'aide de la technologie Advanced Multiforming, n'affiche pas plus de 1030 grammes sur la balance.

Country: Germany · Year: 2012 · Weight: 9.7 kg · Frame: Carbon fiber · Gears: SRAM X.0, 30 speed · Tyres: 29" · Brakes: Magura MT6

SMOOTH WARRIOR

29" MOUNTAINBIKE HOOK, PUNCH CYCLES

Tests by leading magazines highlight the outstanding qualities of the 29" Mountainbike Hook from Punch Cycles. German titanium specialist Mario Sillack has managed to square the circle: the Hook frame is relatively lightweight and extremely solid, and yet it's also a supple and comfortable ride thanks to the superior properties of titanium. As a material, titanium is expensive and considered difficult to work with, but the welds on the Hook—the indicators and proof of quality manufacturing—are flawless ornaments.

Überragende Eigenschaften attestierten Tests führender Magazine dem 29er Mountainbike Hook von Punch Cycles. Dem deutschen Titanspezialisten Mario Sillack gelingt die Quadratur des Kreises: Das 29er Mountainbike Hook besitzt einen relativ leichten und dabei extrem steifen Rahmen, fährt sich jedoch geschmeidig und komfortabel, dank des Edelwerkstoffs Titan. Titan ist als Grundmaterial teuer und gilt als schwer zu verarbeiten. Die Schweißnähte am Hook, Visitenkarte und Zeugen der Herstellungsqualität, sind makellose Schmuckstücke.

Les tests des meilleurs magazines vantent l'excellence du 29" Mountainbike Hook de Punch Cycles. L'Allemand Mario Sillack, spécialiste du titane, a résolu la quadrature du cercle: le Hook, qui dispose d'un cadre relativement léger mais extrêmement rigide, se montre souple et confortable à l'usage grâce à ce noble matériau qu'est le titane. Ce matériau onéreux est réputé difficile à travailler. Les soudures du Hook sont le fruit d'un véritable travail d'orfèvre qui illustre parfaitement la qualité de fabrication.

Country: Germany · Year: 2011 · Weight: 9.8 kg · Frame: Titanium · Gears: 30 · Tyres: 29" · Brakes: Hydraulic disc brakes

DOUBLE THE FUN

JEKYLL, CANNONDALE

The name says it all. With the Jekyll, the American brand Cannondale has managed to build a sensitive full suspension system with perfect climbing properties. With the flick of a lever, the Jekyll changes personality. In "Elevate" mode, with 3.5 inches of travel the Jekyll makes a molehill out of any mountain. Set the special DYAD shock with two air chambers to "Flow" and Dr. Jekyll mutates into a fast, smooth downhiller. The super-light BallisTec carbon material was developed for military applications such as bulletproof vests, so you know it can withstand all the bumps and impacts typically encountered by bike riders.

Der Modellname ist Programm. Die US-Marke Cannondale schafft mit dem Jekyll den Spagat, ein sensibles Fullsuspension mit perfekten Klettereigenschaften zu konstruieren. Mit einem Hebelklick ändert das Jekyll seine Persönlichkeit: Im Modus Elevate mit 90 mm Federweg wird jeder Berg zum Maulwurfshügel. Steht der spezielle DYAD-Dämpfer mit zwei Luftkammern auf Flow, mutiert Dr. Jekyll zum schnellen, problemlosen Downhiller. Das superleichte BallisTec-Carbonmaterial ist eine Entwicklung für den militärischen Einsatz, wie schusssichere Westen, und somit unempfindlich gegen Stöße und Schläge, wie sie im rauen Bike-Alltag vorkommen.

Le nom annonce la couleur. La marque américaine Cannondale réalise ici le grand écart en conférant à ce tout-suspendu de véritables qualités de grimpeur. D'une simple action de manette, le Jekyll change totalement de personnalité: le mode Elevate et ses 90 mm de débattement réduisent les montagnes au rang de simples taupinières. Placé en position Flow, l'amortisseur DYAD change de volume de ressort pneumatique et transforme Dr Jekyll en un descendeur fiable et rapide. Le carbone BallisTec, un matériau ultraléger développé pour des applications militaires comme les gilets pare-balles, est insensible aux chocs et aux impacts auxquels un VTT doit faire face à chaque sortie.

Country: USA · Year: 2010 · Weight: 12.5 kg · Frame: Carbon · Gears: SRAM 2 x 10
Tyres: 26 x 2,4" · Brakes: Avid elixir 9 carbon

MARATHON CHAMPION

R.R2 FS WORLDCUP, ROTWILD

ADP Engineering is constantly earning top marks for its sensitive yet highly effective bike fullsuspension chassis. On the basis of thorough, carefully conceived engineering, this german company based near Frankfurt developed its Rotwild R.R2 FS Worldcup. The stiff but light frame is produced using Module Monocoque Technology. Special features such as the two bottle holders reflect the German developer's racing experience and love of detail—which were rewarded with a World Champion Marathon win and more international successes.

Ein sensibles, aber dabei höchst effektives Fahrwerk bringt der Firma ADP Engineering immer wieder Testsiege. Mit gründlicher und durchdachter Ingenieursarbeit entwickelten die Hessen das Rotwild R.R2 FS Worldcup. Der steife, aber leichte Carbonrahmen wird in aufwendiger modularer Monocoque-Technologie gefertigt. Besonderheiten wie zwei Flaschenhalter zeigen die Rennsporterfahrung und die Liebe zum Detail der deutschen Entwickler. Belohnt wurde dies mit dem Marathon-Weltmeistertitel sowie weiteren internationalen Erfolgen.

ADP Engineering réalise ici une machine sensible, mais redoutablement efficace, qui truste, comme toujours, la première place des tests comparatifs. Les ingénieurs de la firme allemande positionée près de Francfort ont mené un profond travail de réflexion pour élaborer le Rotwild R.R2 FS Worldcup. Le cadre, à la fois léger et rigide, est une application de leur technologie «Monocoque-Modul». Des détails comme ceux des deux bidons témoignent de l'expérience de la course et de l'amour du détail du créateur allemand, qui a remporté un titre de champion du monde de marathon et plusieurs victoires internationales.

Country: Germany · Year: 2012 · Weight: 9.8 kg · Frame: MMT Carbon Modular Monocoque Technique / HM Carbon Fibre · Gears: 20 or 30 · Tyres: 26" · Brakes: Shimano XTR hydraulic disc

URBAN BIKES

CLASSY CITY TOURING

PUBLIC M8 BIKE, PUBLIC

A San Francisco company is building European-inspired bikes. Company founder Rob Forbes is out to make biking as easy and pleasant for his fellow citizens as possible. Inspired by ordinary, everyday bikes from the Old World, PUBLIC emphasizes clean designs, bright colors, sturdy frames, and reliable components. Useful accessories such as baskets and rear racks are intended to make the PUBLIC Bike even more appealing for everyday use.

Ein amerikanisches Unternehmen in San Francisco entwirft Räder nach europäischem Modell: Firmengründer Rob Forbes will seinen Landsleuten das tägliche Radfahren so einfach und angenehm wie möglich machen. Angeregt von Gebrauchsrädern des alten Kontinents, setzt PUBLIC auf klare Gestaltung, frohe Farben, stabile Rahmen und zuverlässige Komponenten. Nützliche Anbauteile wie Körbe und Gepäckträger sollen zum täglichen Gebrauch des PUBLIC Bike verführen.

Voici une entreprise américaine installée à San Francisco qui crée des vélos d'inspiration européenne. Son fondateur, Rob Forbes, veut rendre la vie aussi facile et agréable que possible à ses compatriotes cyclistes. S'inspirant des anciennes machines du vieux continent, PUBLIC Bikes mise sur un équipement simple, des couleurs gaies, des cadres stables et des composants fiables. Les accessoires pratiques comme les paniers et les porte-bagages sont pensés pour un usage quotidien.

Country: USA · Year: 2010 · Weight: 13 kg · Frame: PUBLIC 4130 chromoly steel frame
Gears: Shimano Nexus Inter-8, 8 speed internal geared hub · Tyres: Kenda Kwest,
700 x 35C · Brakes: Alloy dual pivot caliper brake, super long reach (55–73 mm)

THE NEW OLD SCHOOL BIKE

PAULA, RETROVELO

The name says it all: Leipzig-based manufacturer Retrovelo invests a modern design with old-time values, opting for character instead of trendiness—a niche market instead of mass appeal. The elegantly curved down tube, the open fork crown, the cream-colored Schwalbe tires, and the chrome-plated light make Paula an elegant urban companion, whether for a shopping trip or a city cruise.

Der Name ist Programm: Die Leipziger Manufaktur Retrovelo setzt auf alte Werte in moderner Ausführung. Charakter statt Trend, Marktnische statt Massenkompatibilität. Das elegant geschwungene Unterrohr, die durchbrochene Gabelkrone, cremefarbene Schwalbe-Reifen und die verchromte Beleuchtung machen Paula zu einer eleganten Stadtbegleiterin beim Shoppen und City-Cruisen.

Son nom donne le ton: l'entreprise Retrovelo de Leipzig, qui mise sur les valeurs de toujours et une technique d'aujourd'hui, recherche le caractère plutôt que la mode, un marché de niche plutôt que le grand public. La barre supérieure joliment galbée, la tête de fourche ajourée, les pneus Schwalbe couleur crème et les phares chromés font de l'élégante Paula la complice de séances de shopping ou de promenades en ville.

Country: Germany · Year: 2003 · Weight: From 13 to 18.3 kg · Frame: Steel · Gears: Hub circuits and single-speed
Tyres: 26 x 2.35" · Brakes: Hub brake systems

A BRITISH CLASSIC

GUV'NOR, PASHLEY CYCLES

It epitomizes retro. In 1930 Pashley, Great Britain's oldest bicycle manufacturer, was already building the frame for the Guv'nor, called the Path Racer, in historic Stratford-upon-Avon. Features such as Buckingham Black paint, Sturmey Archer drum brakes, gold-lined black rims, cream-colored tires, and the complementary Guv'nor's tea blend radiate British charm. For the lugged frame, only one material will do: Reynolds 531, the best steel alloy available today. The 24.5-inch diamond frame has a striking double top tube.

Der Inbegriff von Retro. Bereits 1930 baute Pashley, die älteste Radmanufaktur Großbritanniens, den Originalrahmen des Guv'nor, genannt Path Racer, im geschichtsträchtigen Stratford-upon-Avon. Features wie die Buckingham-Black-Lackierung, Sturmey-Archer-Trommelbremsen, schwarze Felgen mit Goldrand, cremefarbene Bereifung und die beigegebene Guv'nor-Teemischung verströmen britischen Charme. Für den gemufften Rahmen kommt nur ein Material infrage: Reynolds 531, die beste Stahllegierung von heute. In Größe 24.5 Zoll wird der Diamant-Rahmen mit markantem Doppel-Oberrohr gebaut.

L'incarnation du rétro. En 1930, dans la ville chargée d'histoire de Stratford-upon-Avon, le plus ancien fabricant de cycles de Grande-Bretagne, Pashley, construisait déjà le cadre original du Guv'nor pour un modèle plus ancien: le «Path Racer». Livré avec une sélection de thés appelée Guv'nor, le vélo arbore une peinture Buckingham-Black, des freins à tambours Sturmey-Archer, des jantes noires avec un liseré doré et des pneus crème qui lui confèrent son charme so british. Un seul matériau pouvait se montrer digne de son cadre en acier manchonné: le Reynolds 531, le meilleur alliage d'acier à ce jour. Le cadre de 24,5 pouces en losange reçoit une remarquable double barre horizontale.

Country: United Kingdom · Year: 1930/2007 · Weight: 13 kg · Frame: Reynolds 531
Gears: Single gear, or Sturmey-Archer three-speed gear · Tyres: English 28 x 1 ⅜ " · Brakes: Sturmey-Archer drum brakes (2.75" drum)

GET BACK ON TRACK

FINKLE'S MONOLITH, ICARUS

For Ian Sutton, steel is definitely the most versatile material for frames. The builder learned his craft from Koichi Yamaguchi, and from working at the renowned company Seven, before striking out on his own with Icarus. Now Sutton dabbles with steel's myriad possibilities and is constantly employing new tubes, wall thicknesses, alloys, and tube diameters—whatever is needed or requested by a customer. With its short wheelbase, the Monolith's extravagant design is based on classic track bikes, and its split seat tube is unique in the way it bends back and straddles the rear wheel.

Für Ian Sutton ist Stahl definitiv das variabelste Material für Rahmen. Der Fahrradbauer lernte sein Handwerk bei Koichi Yamaguchi und der renommierten Firma Seven, bevor er sich mit Icarus selbstständig machte. Und so spielt Sutton nun mit allen Möglichkeiten von Stahl und wählt Rohre, Wandstärken, Legierungen, Rohrdurchmesser immer neu nach Anforderung und Kundenwunsch. Das Monolith ist ein extravaganter Entwurf in Anlehnung an klassische Bahnräder mit kurzem Radstand, wobei das geteilte Sitzrohr aus dem Rahmen fällt, indem es das Hinterrad umschwingt.

Pour Ian Sutton, l'acier est vraiment le matériau le plus façonnable qui soit pour un cadre. Le constructeur a fait son apprentissage auprès de Koichi Yamaguchi et de la fameuse société Seven avant de voler de ses propres ailes en fondant Icarus. À chaque commande, Sutton répond aux souhaits de ses clients en jouant avec les diverses possibilités qu'offre l'acier pour choisir l'épaisseur et l'alliage du matériau, ainsi que les tubes et leur diamètre. Le Monolith est une création extravagante s'inspirant des vélos de piste classiques et de leur empattement réduit, qui se caractérise par un double tube de selle courbe qui passe de part et d'autre de la roue arrière.

Country: USA · Year: 2010 · Weight: 8.6 kg · Frame: True Temper VHT steel
Gears: Fixed gear · Tyres: 700 x 23C · Brakes: None

RAW BUT NEAT

DUOMATIC, HAMMARHEAD INDUSTRIES

Hammarhead Industries has already made a name for themselves with stripped Ural and Triumph motorcycles. Their first bicycle design is just as raw, but by no means unsophisticated. The Duomatic takes its name from the Fichtel & Sachs two-speed kick back hub, a few of which were rescued from dusty storerooms. The spare design was inspired by James Hammarhead's Schwinn New World, which like the Duomatic, has a coaster brake and no cables. Hammarhead collaborated with the single-speed builder Iro to produce the matte black frame. The chunky bronze badge on the head tube was created by the artist Adam Smith.

Die Firma Hammarhead Industries machte sich einen Namen mit umgebauten gestrippten Ural- und Triumph-Motorrädern. Ebenso roh, aber keineswegs ungeschlacht ist ihr erster Radentwurf: Das Duomatic hat seinen Namen von den Fichtel-&-Sachs-Zweigangnaben, von denen einige Exemplare aus verstaubten Lagern gerettet wurden. Vorbild war ein Schwinn New World des Firmengründers, das ebenso wie das Duomatic durch die Rücktrittbremse ohne Kabel zum Hinterbau auskommt. In Zusammenarbeit mit der Singlespeed-Schmiede Iro in Pennsylvania entstehen die Rahmen, die mattschwarz beschichtet werden. Die markante Plakette aus Bronze am Steuerrohr ist ein Entwurf des Künstlers Adam Smith.

L'entreprise Hammarhead s'est fait un nom dans la préparation dépouillée de motos Ural et Triumph. Sa première création de vélo est fidèle à son style à la fois brut et sans lourdeur : le Duomatic tire son nom des moyeux deux vitesses Fichtel & Sachs dont quelques exemplaires ont été retrouvés dans quelque atelier poussiéreux. Il s'inspire d'un Schwinn New World ayant appartenu au fondateur de l'entreprise. Comme chez son modèle, un freinage par rétropédalage permet d'éviter tout câble disgracieux sur le triangle arrière. Les cadres à la robe noire mate sont réalisés en collaboration avec Iro, constructeur de Pennsylvanie spécialisé dans les vélos à pignons fixes. La plaquette en bronze sur la douille de direction est la création de l'artiste Adam Smith.

Country: USA · Year: 2012 · Weight: 11 kg · Frame: Heat treated chromoly steel · Gears: 2 speed · Tyres: 25" · Brakes: Coaster

FRESHLY GROUND

RISTRETTO DOPPIO/BLACK 11, CREME BICYCLES

A bike should be like an espresso—a simple everyday object, but each one produced with loving care as a separate little work of art. That's how the Danzig company Creme sees its bikes, all of which are built with steel frames. And the Ristretto Doppio is no exception. It's suitable for city and country riding thanks to low-maintenance components like the gear hub, and the elegantly designed, light stainless steel carrier which, along with the disc brakes, forms a bright contrast to the Ristretto Doppio's classic dark look.

Ein Fahrrad sollte sein wie ein Espresso: einfach und beliebt, doch wenn jeder einzelne mit Liebe und Sorgfalt gemacht wird, ist er ein kleines Kunstwerk. So sieht die Company Creme aus Danzig ihre Räder, die durchweg mit Stahlrahmen gebaut werden. Das Ristretto Doppio macht da keine Ausnahme: stadt- und landtauglich durch wartungsarme Komponenten wie die Nabenschaltung, dazu elegant gestaltete leichte Gepäckträger, die ebenso wie die Scheibenbremsen den hellen Kontrast zum dunklen klassischen Look des Ristretto Doppio bieten.

Un vélo, c'est comme un expresso: simple et délicieux. Et lorsque chacun d'eux est réalisé avec soin et amour, il devient une véritable œuvre d'art. C'est dans cette philosophie que la société Creme de Danzig conçoit ses vélos qui adoptent tous un cadre en acier. Le Ristretto Doppio, qui ne déroge pas à la règle, est à l'aise aussi bien en ville qu'à la campagne grâce à des composants qui requièrent peu d'entretien comme son moyeu à vitesses intégrées. La robe noire classique du cadre et des jantes contrastent avec les légers porte-bagages et les freins à disques.

Country: Poland · Year: 2012 · Weight: 14 kg · Frame: CR-MO steel by Tange
Gears: 11 internal gears – Alfine 11 shimano · Tyres: 28" · Brakes: Shimano Alfine

GERMAN SEDUCTION

LUDWIG XIV, SCHINDELHAUER BIKES

Understatement, not pageantry. The Ludwig XIV, designed by the german company Schindelhauer as a timeless touring bike, has an elegant and unobtrusive presence enhanced by its almost silent Gates belt drive and Rohloff hub. The specially developed slider suspension system on the dropout reflects both sophisticated technology and user-friendliness, and the Brooks leather seat adds a classic touch. In terms of functionality, the Ludwig XIV embodies the philosophy of the Schindelhauer, Holstein, Zehren and Schellhase quartet, whose bikes have earned them multiple awards.

Understatement statt Pomp: Der als zeitloser Tourer konzipierte Ludwig XIV der Magdeburger Firma Schindelhauer präsentiert sich elegant und unauffällig durch den nahezu lautlosen Gates-Riemenantrieb und die Rohloff-Nabe. Das speziell entwickelte Slider-Spannsystem am Ausfallende besticht durch ausgefeilte Technik und Bedienfreundlichkeit. Klassik-Reminiszenz stellt lediglich der Brooks-Ledersattel dar. Ludwig XIV steht in seiner Funktionalität für die Philosophie des Quartetts Schindelhauer, Zehren, Holstein und Schellhase, dessen Räder mehrfach preisgekrönt sind.

La prestance plutôt que le faste. La compagnie allemande Schindelhauer a conçu le Ludwig XIV, le roi soleil de la bicyclette, une vélo urbain indémodable, élégant et discret. Le silence presque absolu de l'entraînement par courroie, le moyeu Rohloff à vitesses intégrées et le système de pattes de tension spécialement conçu témoignent d'une technique parfaitement chiadée et séduisent par leur simplicité d'utilisation, tandis que la selle en cuir Brooks apporte une touche de classicisme. Par sa fonctionnalité, le Ludwig XIV est fidèle aux principes du quartet formé par Schindelhauer, Zehren, Holstein et Schellhase, dont les cycles ont remporté de nombreux prix.

Country: Germany · Year: 2011 · Weight: 11.9 kg · Frame: Aluminum · Gears: Rohloff Speedhub 14 gears
Tyres: Continental Grand Prix 4-Season 28-622 · Brakes: Shimano disc brakes

HEROES OF THE PAST

ALLEY, VELOHELD

Three Dresden designers and bike freaks created the veloheld brand to commemorate their heroes from biking history, such as Olaf Ludwig and Michael Hübner. The Alley is the perfect embodiment of the young company's philosophy: a plain single-speed bike with a classic CroMoly steel frame and cool track cranks. The paintwork is likewise modest and understated. The Alley is a straightforward, functional, uncomplicated bike stripped down to the bare essentials.

Drei Dresdner Designer und Radfanatiker stehen hinter der deutschen Marke veloheld, benannt in Reminiszenz an ihre Heroes der Radhistorie wie Olaf Ludwig und Michael Hübner. Das Alley verkörpert die Philosophie der jungen Company: ein schlichter Singlespeeder mit klassischem CroMoly-Stahlrahmen und coolen Track-Kurbeln. Die Lackierung ist ebenso zurückhaltend und transportiert den Understatement-Gedanken. Das Alley ist pur, funktionell und problemlos, reduziert auf das Notwendige an einem Rad.

Trois designers de Dresde, tous fondus de vélo, sont à l'origine de la marque allemande veloheld, dont le nom rend hommage aux héros de la petite reine comme Olaf Ludwig et Michael Hübner. L'Alley incarne parfaitement la philosophie de la jeune entreprise: un simple mono-vitesse avec cadre classique en acier CroMoly et manivelles de pédalier de pistard. La robe, tout aussi sobre, véhicule une certaine idée de la finition. Pur, fonctionnel et sans contraintes, l'Alley se limite à l'essentiel sur un vélo.

Country: Germany · Year: 2007 · Weight: 9.3 kg · Frame: Double butted CrMo · Gears: Singlespeed · Tyres: 28" · Brakes: 2 caliper brakes

PURE THOUGHTS

COLUMBUS MS TRACK BIKE , BISHOP BIKES

The Columbus MS Track Bike was voted best steel bike at the renowned North American Handmade Bicycle Show (NAHBS) 2011 in Austin. Chris Bishop, owner and head of Bishop Bikes in Baltimore, doesn't just build bikes. He creates unique steel pieces, each with a different background and character. This daring blue and green track bike is a classic example of a Fixie bike: super-short wheelbase, extremely deep-drawn stem, and a delicate, flawless frame made from an Italian Columbus tubeset.

Bei der renommierten North American Handmade Bicycle Show NAHBS 2011 in Austin wurde das Columbus MS Track Bike als bestes Stahlbike ausgezeichnet. Chris Bishop, Besitzer und Chef von Bishop Bikes in Baltimore, baut nicht einfach Räder, er kreiert Einzelstücke in Stahl, jedes davon mit anderem Hintergrund und Charakter. Das gewagte blau-grüne Track Bike ist ein klassischer Vertreter der Fixie-Bahnräder: superkurzer Radstand, extrem tiefgezogener Vorbau und ein filigraner, makelloser Rahmen aus italienischem Columbus-Rohrsatz.

En 2011, lors du fameux NAHBS, le salon nord-américain du vélo fait main de Austin, le Columbus MS Track Bike a reçu le prix du meilleur vélo en acier. Chris Bishop, patron de Bishop Bikes, n'est pas un simple constructeur de vélos. Il crée à Baltimore des pièces uniques en acier, chacune d'elles possédant un caractère propre à son histoire. Ce Track Bike, qui ose une livrée bleue et verte, est un digne représentant des vélos de piste à pignon fixe: empattement réduit au maximum, potence plongeante et un cadre élancé, impeccable, constitué de tubes italiens signés Columbus.

Country: USA · Year: 2011 · Weight: 7.5 kg · Frame: Columbus Cyclex Steel Multishaped Tube Set
Gears: Singlespeed · Tyres: 700C · Brakes: None

STREET MUSICIAN

BERLINO, PASCULLI

What do you get when an oboist/passionate racing cyclist and a Berlin bike nerd found a bike company together? A name that sounds like music. Pasculli was a Sicilian musician known as "The Paganini of the Oboe." In Germany's capital city, Christoph Hartmann and Maik Kresse, together with designer Andreas Töpfer, create bikes that are the embodiment of elegance and Italy's passion for cycling. The Berlino is a slender single speed built with fine Dedacciai tubing whose nimble handling makes it ideal for the cities of this world.

Was entsteht, wenn ein Oboist und leidenschaftlicher Rennradfahrer mit einem Berliner Bike-Tüftler eine Radfirma gründet? Ein Name wie Musik. Pasculli ist ein sizilianischer Musiker, der als „Paganini der Oboe" galt. Christoph Hartmann und Maik Kresse verwirklichen zusammen mit Designer Andreas Töpfer in Deutschlands Hauptstadt Räder, die die Eleganz und Leidenschaft Italiens für den Radsport transportieren. Das Berlino ist ein schlankes Singlespeed aus feinem Dedacciai-Rohr und durch sein agiles Fahrverhalten wie geschaffen für die Metropolen dieser Welt.

Prenez un coureur cycliste passionné et joueur de hautbois; associez-le à un monteur de vélos berlinois et laissez-les fonder une marque de cycles. Le résultat s'appelle Pasculli, en hommage au virtuose sicilien, sorte de «Paganini du hautbois». Au cœur de la capitale allemande du vélo, Christoph Hartmann et Maik Kresse créent, avec le designer Andreas Töpfer, des vélos qui respirent l'élégance et la passion italienne du cyclisme. Le Berlino est une monture agile à une seule vitesse, conçue avec les meilleurs tubes de la marque Dedacciai, pour les rues des métropoles de ce monde.

Country: Germany/Italy · Year: 2009 · Weight: 7.5 kg · Frame: Aluminum
Gears: Single speed and fixed (2 gears) · Tyres: 28" · Brakes: Miche

A CLASSICAL REMINDER

GRASS TRACK, TOWNSEND

Framebuilder Gregory Townsend's Grass Track commemorates the almost forgotten sport of grass track racing. The slender steel bike with an incredibly sweet paint job by Joe Bell signals the return of the classic track racer with its short wheelbase. Townsend was born in Britain but now lives in California. One of his trademarks is the elegant handlebar-stem unit. The light coloured Ghisallo beech rims and leather bar wrap say "retro," as do the Campagnolo Record Pista components.

Rahmenbauer Gregory Townsend erinnert mit seinem Grass Track an die nahezu vergessene Disziplin der Rennen auf dem Rasen-Oval. Schlank in Stahl, mit unglaublich liebevoller Lackierung von Joe Bell, ist das Grass Track die Wiedergeburt des klassischen Bahn-Rads mit kurzem Radstand. Eines der Markenzeichen von Townsend, gebürtiger Brite und in Kalifornien lebend, ist die elegante Lenker-Vorbau-Einheit. Die hellen Ghisallo-Felgen aus Buchenholz und das Lenkerband aus Leder unterstreichen den Retro-Charakter ebenso wie die Campa Record Pista-Komponenten.

Avec ce Grass Track, le constructeur de cadre britannique Gregory Townsend, installé en Californie, ravive le souvenir presque disparu de ces courses sur pistes ovales recouvertes d'herbe. Le Grass Track est la renaissance du vélo de piste classique en acier et à empattement court. L'émotion que suscite la finesse du cadre et la peinture signée Joe Bell est renforcée par un élégant ensemble cintre-potence, véritable marque de fabrique de Townsend. Les jantes Ghisallo en bois de hêtre clair et le cuir qui habille le cintre soulignent le caractère rétro, tout comme les composants Campagnolo Record Pista.

Country: USA · Year: 2007 · Weight: 7 kg · Frame: Dedacciai steel · Gears: Fixed gear 48-17 Tyres: 28" Tubular Cyclo Cross

RETRO-INSPIRED MODERN

TICINO 20D, ELECTRA BICYCLE COMPANY

A modern interpretation of European hand built bicycles of the '40s and '50s. With its Ticino 20D, Electra combines classic craftsmanship design with a highly practical approach. Details such as a lugged fork with chrome-plated investment-cast crown, a compact double alloy chain ring, hammered fenders, classic touring pedals that accept toe clips with leather straps, and comfortable backswept handlebars with reverse-hinged bar-end brake levers emphasize its historical influences. A responsive, lightweight aluminum frame and 20-speed Shimano components along with Five Star high flange hubset are part of the Ticino 20D's hidden modern side.

Ein Retro-Stadtrad im Cruiser Style mit Anleihen von europäischen Rädern aus den Vierzigern und Fünfzigern. Elektra verbindet sein California Design mit praktischen Aspekten am Ticino 20D. Details wie unten liegende Schalthebel, eine gemuffte Gabel, gehämmerte Schutzbleche, klassische Rennpedale mit Haken und Riemen und ein weit geschwungener komfortabler Lenker mit Lenkerstopfen-Bremshebeln unterstreichen den historisch angehauchten Charakter. Ein leichter Aluminiumrahmen, eine Shimano-Schaltung mit 20 Gängen und leichtlaufende Hochflansch-Naben sind die versteckte moderne Seite des Ticino 20D.

Un vélo de ville rétro avec une touche de custom et des emprunts aux vélos européens des années 40 et 50. Elektra synthétise dans ce Ticino 20D de nombreux aspects pratiques dans un design californien. Le Ticino 20D affiche un caractère historique que soulignent les courbes généreuses d'un confortable guidon équipé de leviers de freins inversés, mais aussi des détails comme ses leviers de vitesse, ses garde-boues martelés, ainsi que ses pédales de course classiques avec cale-pieds et sangles. Toutefois, son cadre en aluminium léger, son groupe Shimano 20 vitesses et ses moyeux grandes flasques témoignent pour leur part d'une modernité discrète.

Country: USA · Year: 2010 · Weight: 17 kg · Frame: 6061-T6 Butted Alloy · Gears: 20 · Tyres: 700C · Brakes: Tektro Cantilever

YOU ARE YOUR OWN BIKE

SINGLESPEED, URBIKE

Advertiser Mike Glaser and bike freak Robin Homolac let bike lovers create their own designs. They simply provide the standard Urbike hardware in the form of a classic welded steel frame. Using the web configurator or in urbike stores, customers select colors for the frame, rims, and components. Thus, every Urbike is a one-of-a-kind, customized city bike ideal for design- and quality-conscious urban bike fans. With the Urbike, the Munich-based company is also celebrating the comeback of the kick shift hub gear: the Sturmey Archer 2-speed kick shift hub doesn't in any way detract from the purist look.

Der Werber Mike Glaser und der Fahrrad-Freak Robin Homolac lassen dem Radfan freie Auswahl in der Gestaltung. Sie liefern die Hardware des Urbike – klassische geschweißte Stahlrahmen. Im Web-Konfigurator und in den Urbike Shops in München und in Hamburg wählt der Kunde seine Farben für Rahmen, Felgen, Komponenten. So ist jedes Urbike ein Unikat, ein individualisiertes Citybike für designorientierte und qualitätsbewusste urbane Fahrradfans. Du bist dein Fahrrad. Die Münchner feiern mit dem Urbike auch die Renaissance der Rücktrittschaltung: Eine Sturmey-Archer-Kick-Shift-Nabe arbeitet in der Duospeed-Ausführung, ohne den puristischen Look zu beeinträchtigen.

Mike Glaser, publicitaire, et Robin Homolac, passionné de vélos, laissent aux fans de la petite reine une totale liberté de choix pour l'équipement. Ils fournissent la base de l'Urbike: un cadre classique en acier moulé. Un outil de configuration disponible en magasin et sur internet permet à leurs clients aussi exigeants sur la qualité que sur le design, de choisir en ligne la couleur du cadre, des jantes et de l'équipement, faisant de chaque Urbike un vélo urbain unique. Les deux Munichois célèbrent également la renaissance du changement de vitesse par rétropédalage avec un moyeu Sturmey-Archer Kick Shift à deux vitesses intégrées qui préserve les lignes pures de leur modèle.

Country: Germany · Year: 2010 · Weight: 11 kg · Frame: Steel · Gears: 1 and 2 · Tyres: 28" · Brakes: Urbike by Tektron

LA DONNA MOBILE

MOSCOVA, BELLA CIAO

The German-Italian workshop of Bella Ciao produces only five Moscova bikes a year. The all-chrome-plated frame of the women's bike is entirely hand-built in Northern Italy, but finished and assembled in Germany. As a special highlight, the Moscova is also available with the seat and handlebar grips in stingray leather. Bella Ciao—the name comes from a historic Italian partisan song—specializes in timelessly elegant bicycles with a traditional Italian flair, and every year comes out with a limited series.

Nur fünf Moscova-Räder pro Jahr stellt die deutsch-italienische Schmiede Bella Ciao her. Der vollverchromte Rahmen des Damenrads wird in Norditalien komplett handgefertigt und in Deutschland vervollständigt. Die besondere Note verleiht dem Moscova auf Wunsch ein Bezug aus Rochenhaut auf Sattel und Griffen. Bella Ciao – der Firmenname rührt von einem historischen italienischen Partisanenlied – hat sich auf zeitlos elegante Räder mit traditionellem italienischem Flair spezialisiert und legt jedes Jahr eine limitierte Serie auf.

Le fabricant germano-italien Bella Ciao ne produit que cinq Moscova chaque année. Le cadre de ce vélo pour femme, entièrement chromé, est entièrement fabriqué dans le nord de l'Italie et équipé en Allemagne. Le galuchat, disponible sur commande, recouvre la selle et les poignées, conférant au Moscova une touche unique. Bella Ciao – la société tire son nom de la chanson populaire adoptée par les partisans italiens – s'est spécialisée dans la production en série limitée de bicyclettes élégants, hors du temps, et dotés d'un charme bien italien.

Country: Germany/Italy · Year: 2011 · Weight: From 11 kg
Frame: Columbus steel · Gears: Optional · Tyres: 28" · Brakes: Front and rear Caliper brakes

BACK TO THE FUTURE

BIRDIE, BOBBIN BIKES

A British bike brand is building modern bikes in a totally retro design. Although this classically-styled women's bike "Birdie" looks as if it has come right out of the 70's, it's actually a contemporary model with an old-school look. The fully lugged frame has 26-inch wheels that render the Birdie agile and flexible. The gear ratio of the robust Sturmey Archer 3-speed hub is equal to any shopping trip, and the elevated seat position ensures a comprehensive view over city traffic.

Die britische Marke baut moderne Räder im absoluten Retro-Design. Obwohl das klassische Damenrad Birdie aussieht wie aus den Siebzigern, ist es ein aktuelles Modell im Old-School-Look. Im komplett gemufften Rahmen stecken 26-Zoll-Laufräder, was das Birdie agil und wendig macht. Die Übersetzung der unverwüstlichen Sturmey-Archer-Dreigangnabe genügt für alle Shopping-Touren und die aufrechte Sitzposition sorgt für Überblick im Stadtverkehr.

La marque britannique réalise des vélos modernes dans le plus pur style rétro. Bien que ce vélo femme classique semble tout droit sorti des années 70, le Birdie est un modèle actuel dans une robe old school. Maniable et agile, il associe des roues de 26 pouces à un cadre à manchons. La transmission de l'inusable moyeu Sturmey-Archer à trois vitesses intégrées suffit amplement pour les sorties shopping. La position de conduite haute et droite est bien commode en circulation.

Country: United Kingdom · Year: 2011 · Weight: 14 kg · Frame: Hi-ten and chromoly steel
Gears: 3 · Tyres: 26 x 1 ⅜ " · Brakes: Tektro caliper

NOBLE METAL

NO.1, PAUL BUDNITZ

Kidrobot founder Paul Budnitz was looking for the perfect commuting bike. When he didn't find it, he set up his own company and created the No.1, a city bike with an all-titanium frame welded by Lynskey, specialists in Tennessee. Even the handlebars, stem, and seat post are made of this lightweight, indestructible precious metal. With its flawless workmanship, internal cables, and high-end components from White Industries and Paul Components, the No.1 is a lifelong companion. According to Budnitz, the curved frame with split seat stays embodies a "timeless design, similar to a classic Aston Martin or Maserati from the '80s."

Der Kidrobot-Gründer Paul Budnitz wollte das perfekte Commuter-Rad. Da er es nicht fand, gründete er eine eigene Firma und kreierte das No.1: ein City-Bike komplett aus Titan, geschweißt von den Spezialisten Lynskey in Tennessee. Selbst Lenker, Vorbau und Sattelstütze bestehen aus dem unzerstörbaren leichten Edelmetall. Makellose Verarbeitung, interne Zugverlegung, High-End-Komponenten von White Industries und Paul Components machen das No.1 zum lebenslangen Begleiter. Der geschwungene Rahmen mit geteilten Sitzstreben verkörpert laut Budnitz ein „zeitloses Design, ähnlich klassischen Aston Martins und Maseratis aus den Achtzigern".

Paul Budnitz, le fondateur de Kidrobot, cherchait le vélo idéal pour les navetteurs. N'ayant rien trouvé de probant, il a fondé sa propre entreprise pour créer le No.1: un vélo urbain entièrement en titane, soudé par le spécialiste Lynskey installé au Tennessee. Même le guidon, la potence et le tube de selle sont façonnés dans ce métal noble, aussi léger qu'indestructible. Avec une finition impeccable, le passage des câbles dans le cadre et des composants griffés High-End de White Industries ou Paul Budnitz, le No.1 est un compagnon pour la vie. Le cadre tout en courbe dans le prolongement des deux haubans produisent selon Budnitz un «design hors du temps, dans la tradition des Aston Martin et des Maserati des années 80».

Country: USA · Year: 2011 · Weight: 8.56 kg · Frame: Titanium · Gears: Single-speed or Internal 11 speed · Tyres: 700C · Brakes: Disc brakes

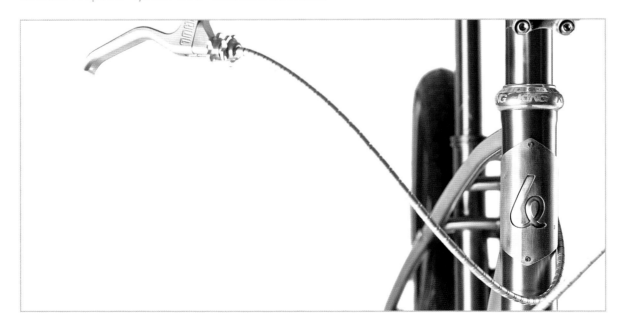

TRUE AMERICAN CRUISER

SPYDER GT, KEITH ANDERSON

Four years of hand-crafting and the use of select exotic materials have made Keith Anderson's Spyder GT a unique work of art. The Oregon-based frame restorer sets up a contrast between the components and the flawless luster of the Tahiti-Blue frame. The red Magura disc brakes, the hand-shaped fenders, and the chain guard made from paduak and wenge wood with paua-shell inlay enhance the visual appeal. A youth bike, the Spyder GT was inspired by his three sons but clearly became too beautiful to fulfill its original purpose.

Vier Jahre Handarbeit und die Verwendung ausgesuchter exotischer Materialien machen das Spyder GT von Keith Anderson zu einem einmaligen Kunstwerk. Der Rahmenrestaurator aus Oregon setzt mit den Komponenten Kontraste zum makellos schimmernden Tahiti-Blau des Rahmens. Die roten Magura-Scheibenbremsen, die handgefertigten Schutzbleche und der Kettenschutz aus den Edelhölzern Paduak und Wenge mit Paua-Perlmuttintarsien sorgen für optische Reize. Ein Jugendrad, inspiriert von seinen drei Söhnen, das eindeutig zu schön für seinen Zweck wurde.

Quatre ans de travail et des matériaux exotiques soigneusement sélectionnés font du Spyder GT de Keith Anderson une œuvre unique. Le restaurateur de cadres, installé dans l'Oregon, recherche la séduction par les contrastes des composants, jouant d'une part sur le bleu brillant de la peinture impeccable du cadre et d'autre part sur le rouge des étriers de freins Magura. Les garde-boues faits main et le carter, réalisés en bois de Padouk et en wengé, sont incrustés de nacre de Paua. Ce vélo de garçon, inspiré par les trois fils de son créateur, est devenu bien trop beau pour remplir ses fonctions originales.

Country: USA · Year: 2009 · Weight: 12 kg · Frame: 4130 Chromoly · Gears: Singlespeed
Tyres: 24" · Brakes: Magura discs with carbon levers

GONE IN 10 SECONDS

STRIDA, STRIDA

When it was released, it was known as the "Wonder Bike." In the course of 100 years of bicycle history, the Strida embodies the first truly new concept for folding bikes, based on one of the world's simplest and sturdiest geometric shapes: the triangle. This bike—weighing a mere 19.84 pounds—has seen several improvements since its initial introduction in 1987. In just ten seconds, it's ready to ride. All the cables are inside the frame, and the Kevlar belt drive is greaseless. Even when folded, it still rolls along on its own wheels.

Als es erschien, nannte man es das „Bike-Wunder". Nach 100 Jahren Fahrrad-Ära war das Strida das erste wirklich neue Konzept für ein Faltrad, basierend auf einer der einfachsten und stabilsten geometrischen Formen der Welt: dem Dreieck. Seit der ersten Präsentation 1987 wurde das nur zehn Kilo wiegende Faltrad weiter verbessert. In nur zehn Sekunden ist es fahrbereit. Alle Züge verlaufen im Rahmen, der Kevlar-Riemenantrieb funktioniert fettfrei. Zusammengeklappt rollt man es auf seinen Rädchen.

Lors de sa sortie, on l'appelait le «Wonder bike». Après un siècle de bicyclettes, le Strida apparaissait comme le premier concept de vélo pliant véritablement nouveau, reprenant l'une des formes géométriques les plus simples et les plus stables au monde: le triangle. Depuis sa présentation en 1987, ce vélo de 10 kg seulement n'a eu de cesse de s'améliorer. Il se déploie désormais en 10 secondes, tous ses câbles passent dans le cadre et la transmission par courroie en Kevlar n'a besoin d'aucun graissage. Replié, il roule toujours sur ses deux roues.

Country: United Kingdom · Year: 1987 · Weight: 10 kg · Frame: 7000 Series aluminum
Gears: Single, 2 speed, and 3 speed · Tyres: 1.5" · Brakes: Mechanical disc brakes

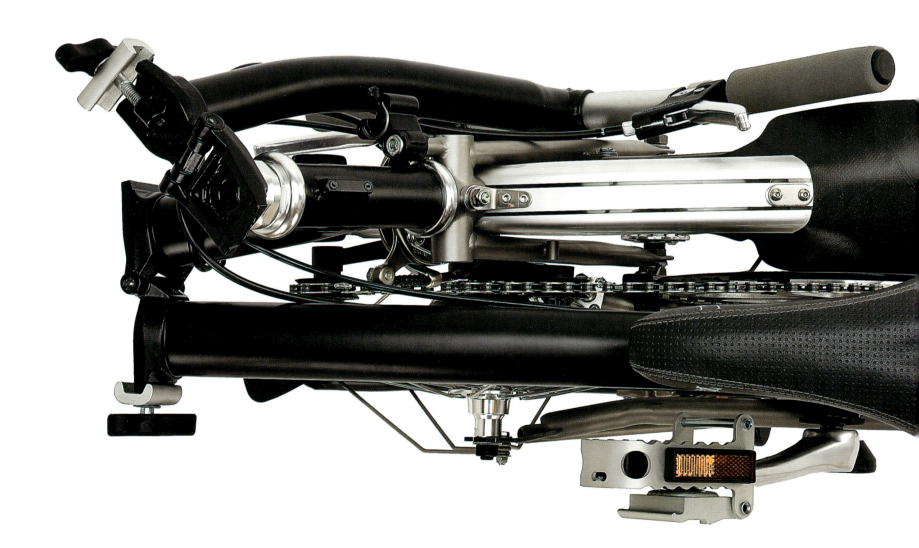

THE TAKE-AWAY-BIKE

M6L-X, BROMPTON

The Brompton brand has become synonymous with folding bikes. This British company has been building their eye-catching, stable bikes with 16-inch wheels and an innovative folding system since the 1980s. The M6L-X is equipped with the six-speed Brompton Wide Range hub. The steel main frame and titanium front fork, rear frame and fender stays, make it more than a kilogram lighter than the standard model. It's the perfect expression of Brompton's philosophy of independence and freedom.

Die Marke Brompton wurde zum Synonym für Falträder. Seit den Achtzigern baut die britische Firma die auffälligen, stabilen Räder mit 16-Zoll-Bereifung und einem innovativen Faltsystem. Das M6L-X ist mit der 6-Gang-Brompton-Wide-Range-Schaltnabe ausgestattet. Der Vorderrahmen aus Stahl, die Titangabel, Rückrahmen und das Schutzblech machen diese Version über ein Kilo leichter als die Standardausführung. Die perfekte Verkörperung der Brompton-Philosophie: Unabhängigkeit und Freiheit zu ermöglichen.

La marque Brompton est devenue synonyme de vélo pliant. Depuis les années 80, la marque britannique d'Andrew Ritchie construit des vélos remarquables de stabilité, présentant des pneus 16 pouces et un système de pliage astucieux. Le M6L-X est équipé d'un moyeu Brompton Wide Range 6 vitesses. Cette version bénéficie de pièces en titane, dont la fourche, le cadre arrière et le garde-boue, qui allègent le vélo de plus d'un kilogramme par rapport à la version standard. La quintessence de la philosophie Brompton: offrir indépendance et liberté.

Country: United Kingdom · Year: 2011 · Weight: 10.7 kg · Frame: Steel
Gears: 6 · Tyres: 16" · Brakes: Brompton Dual Pivot Caliper

MAGIC CARPET

GRASSHOPPER FX, HP VELOTECHNIK

HP Velotechnik, a recognized German specialist in recumbent bikes, combines two systems in the GrassHopper fx. This speedy recumbent bike can be folded to the smallest packing size, making it the ideal traveling companion on epic tours. The rear suspension with 110 mm travel ensures safe riding and is easy on the vertebrae. Development engineer Daniel Pulvermüller has reduced the GrassHopper's weight to just over 15 kg. HP Velotechnik produces its prize-winning model in a small but distinguished workshop near Frankfurt.

HP Velotechnik, anerkannter deutscher Spezialist für Liegeräder, verbindet beim GrassHopper fx zwei Systeme. Das schnelle Liegerad lässt sich auf kleinstes Packmaß zusammenklappen und wird so der ideale Reisegefährte für epische Touren. Die hintere Schwinge weist 110 Millimeter Federweg auf, dies bringt Fahrsicherheit und schont die Bandscheiben. Entwicklungsingenieur Daniel Pulvermüller reduzierte das Gewicht des GrassHopper auf knapp über 15 Kilogramm. In einer kleinen, feinen Manufaktur bei Frankfurt fertigt HP Velotechnik seine preisgekrönten Modelle.

HP Velotechnik, le spécialiste allemand du vélo couché, réunit dans ce GrassHopper fx deux concepts: le vélo couché et le vélo pliant. Replié, il devient le véhicule idéal pour les plus épiques des voyages. Daniel Pulvermüller, l'ingénieur qui a développé le GrassHopper, a ramené son poids à presque 15 kg. Avec un débattement de 110 mm, la suspension arrière garantit un bon comportement routier tout en ménageant la colonne vertébrale. HP Velotechnik, qui a été primée pour ce modèle, fabrique ses vélos dans sa petite usine près de Francfort.

Country: Germany · Year: 2008 · Weight: 15.3 kg · Frame: Aluminum 7005
Gears: 27 speed, combined hub gear and derrailleur gear system · Tyres: 20" · Brakes: V-brakes or disc brakes

URBAN CHIC

IF MODE FOLDING BIKE, PACIFIC CYCLES

The Pacific IF Mode combines clear design with smooth function. In a mere 3 seconds, it can be transformed into a zippy city bike designed by Mark Sanders and engineers Ryan Carroll and Michael Lin. The drivetrain contains a 2-speed hub and is fully enclosed, to stay clean and maintenance-free. The S-shaped frame and the 26-inch wheels guarantee a comfortable ride for the urban commuter.

Das Pacific IF Mode verbindet klares Design und einwandfreie Funktion. Lediglich 3 Sekunden dauert die Verwandlung zum schnittigen Stadtrad, designt von Mark Sanders und den Ingenieuren Ryan Carroll und Michael Lin. Das 2-Gang-Getriebe und der Antrieb sind komplett integriert und somit wartungsfrei. Der S-förmige Hauptrahmen und die 26-Zoll-Laufräder garantieren eine komfortable Fahrt für den Pendler.

Le Pacific IF Mode, développé par Mark Sanders, Ryan Carroll et Michael Lin, associe design aux lignes claires et utilisation facile. 3 secondes suffisent pour le transformer en un petit bolide urbain. La transmission 2 vitesses entièrement intégrée pour éviter toute salissure ne requiert aucun entretien. Le cadre en S et les roues de 26 pouces offrent un confort d'utilisation appréciable pour les navetteurs.

Country: Taiwan · Year: 2009 · Weight: 14.7 kg · Frame: Aluminum · Gears: 2 · Tyres: 26" · Brakes: Mechanical disc brakes

OUT OF THE BOX

BERNDS FALTRAD / TANDEM + BOX BY BERNDS, BERNDS

Thomas Bernds has been building self-designed folding bikes since 1991. The single-tube frame is in one piece, while the swing arm, handlebars, and seat post fold. A belt drive, disc brakes, and fenders make the Bernds single Faltrad suitable for everyday use. The Box is part of a marketing concept whereby customers can experience the advantages of the Faltrad by riding a test bike. The Falttandem provides double the biking fun with its spring-loaded swing arm and sturdy 20-inch wheels furnished with Schwalbe Big Apple tires. The frame has an extremely stable design and is universally usable, thanks to separately adjustable captain and stoker positions. With its short wheelbase, the Bernds tandem is more maneuverable than a traditional tandem.

Thomas Bernds baut Falträder seit 1991 in eigenem Design. Der Einrohr-Rahmen ist ungeteilt, beim Falten werden Schwinge, Lenkerrohr und Sattelrohr eingefahren. Bei Bernds Single-Faltrad sorgen Riemenantrieb, Scheibenbremsen und Schutzbleche für Alltagstauglichkeit. Die Box ist Teil eines Marketingkonzepts, bei dem Kunden mit einem Testrad die Vorteile im Praxistest erradeln können. Doppelten Fahrspaß bieten die Falttandems mit gefederter Schwinge und stabilen 20-Zoll-Laufrädern mit Schwalbes Big-Apple-Bereifung. Der Rahmen ist extrem stabil ausgelegt und durch die getrennt für Captain und Stoker verstellbaren Positionen universell einsetzbar. Durch den kurzen Radstand ist es wendiger als klassische Tandems.

La société allemande Bernds propose d'unir la commodité du vélo pliant et le plaisir de rouler à deux. Ce tandem reprend le bras oscillant suspendu des vélos pliants classiques, ainsi que les roues de 20 pouces remarquables de stabilité, équipées de pneus Schwalbe Big Apple. Le cadre, extrêmement stable lui aussi, est adaptable grâce au réglage séparé des positions de conduite du capitaine (pilote) et du stoker (personne à l'arrière). L'empattement réduit rend le Bernds bien plus maniable que les tandems classiques. Replié, il peut être aisément placé dans un coffre de voiture ou emporté dans les transports en commun.

Country: Germany · Year: 1991 / 1999 · Weight: 9.6 kg / 19.6 kg · Frame: Steel
Gears: From 2 to 24 · Tyres: 20" · Brakes: Rim brakes / Disc brake

UTILITY BIKES

TAXI TO THE PLAYGROUND

LIGHT, CHRISTIANIA BIKES

The Danish original. In 1984, Lars Engstrom built his first three-wheeled bicycle, designed for child transport, as a birthday present for his partner Annie Lerche when the two of them were living in a commune in Copenhagen's alternative, car-free district Christiania. The astonishingly manoeuvrable three-wheeler also turned out to be the perfect basis for a transportation bike. The Classic model, which received the prestigious Danish Classical Prize for 2010/2011, is now built in various different models, including a rickshaw, in a small factory on the Isle of Bornholm, and sold all over the world.

Das dänische Original. Lars Engstrom baute 1984 sein erstes Dreirad zum Transport der Kinder als Geburtstagsgeschenk für seine Partnerin Annie Lerche. Beide lebten in einer Kommune in Kopenhagens alternativem, autofreien Stadtteil Christiania. Das erstaunlich wendige Dreirad erwies sich auch als perfekte Basis für ein Transportbike. Der Klassiker, der 2010/2011 den renommierten Dänischen Classical-Preis erhielt, wird inzwischen in zahlreichen Varianten, sogar als Rikscha, in einer kleinen Manufaktur auf der Insel Bornholm gebaut und in die ganze Welt verkauft.

L'authentique triporteur danois. En 1984, Lars Engstrom a réalisé le premier modèle à l'occasion de l'Anniversaire de sa compagne Annie Lerche pour transporter plus aisément leurs enfants dans Christiania, quartier libertaire et sans voiture de Copenhague, où la famille vivait dans une communauté. Étonnamment agile, le tricycle s'est aussi révélé être la plateforme idéale pour un vélo cargo. Il est aujourd'hui décliné en plusieurs modèles, comme le Rikscha, tous construits dans un atelier de l'île de Bornholm. Au Danemark, la version classique a été récompensée par le célèbre « Classics Prize » 2010/2011.

Country: Denmark · Year: 2000 · Weight: 35 kg · Frame: Alloy (steel also avaible)
Gears: Shimano 7 speed · Tyres: 24" · Brakes: Disc brakes (front); coaster (rear)

KIDS ON TOUR

CARRYO FAMILY, CARRYO

The ecofriendly family outing is now as easy as pie. Instead of having to lift the kids over high crate sides, the Carryo's user-friendly protective frame opens upward with the help of a hydraulically damped gas spring. The transport drum has room for two children. This clever innovation won the Berlin-based Carryo Family the coveted Eurobike Award. The three-wheeled child transporter has axle-pivot steering and also comes in an e-motor version.

Der umweltfreundliche Familienausflug wird zum Kinderspiel. Statt den Nachwuchs über hohe Kistenwände heben zu müssen, öffnet sich beim Carryo freundlich der Schutzrahmen nach oben, unterstützt durch eine Gasdruckfeder. Zwei Kinder haben Platz in der Transport-Trommel. Das Berliner Carryo Family erhielt für diesen innovativen Ansatz den begehrten Eurobike Award. Der dreirädrige Kindertransporter besitzt eine Achsschenkel-Lenkung und wird auch in einer Variante mit E-Motor gebaut.

Même sans voiture, la sortie en famille devient un jeu d'enfant avec ce triporteur berlinois équipé d'un essieu directionnel et, en option, d'un moteur électrique. De plus, au lieu de présenter de hautes parois qui obligent à hisser les enfants hors de la caisse, le Carryo adopte un cadre de protection qui s'élève à l'aide d'un vérin à gaz pour accéder sans peine au coffre réservant suffisamment de place pour deux enfants. Cette innovation a valu au Carryo Family le très convoité Eurobike-Award.

Country: Germany · Year: 2012 · Weight: 32 kg · Frame: Steel · Gears: Shimano Alfine 11 Gears
Tyres: 20" (front); 26" (rear) · Brakes: Magura BIG disc brakes (front); Magura HS33 (rear)

HEAVY LOADED

DUTCH DELIGHT, JOHNNY LOCO

These two bikes represent two new interpretations of the classic cargo theme. The frame of the Dutch Delight—from the Amsterdam bike company Johnny Loco—is made entirely of aluminum. Concern for riding safety yielded an innovative approach: the rear section of the frame leans into the curves, thus eliminating the conventional tricycle's tendency to tip. With the Dutch Delight, shopping with two children is a breeze. The beach cruiser elegantly combines the casual design of a California cruiser with a robust, integrated carrier in front of the handlebars.

Das Cargo-Thema in zwei Formen neu interpretiert. Der Rahmen des Dutch Delight der Amsterdamer Radfirma Johnny Loco besteht komplett aus Aluminium. Fahrsicherheit bringt ein innovativer Ansatz: Der hintere Rahmenteil neigt sich in Kurven, sodass das Kippverhalten üblicher Dreiräder nicht auftritt. Mit dem Dutch Delight ist ein Einkauf mit zwei Kindern kein Problem. Der Beachcruiser verbindet elegant das entspannte Design kalifornischer Cruiser mit einem stabilen integrierten Lastenträger vor dem Lenker.

Le concept de transport à vélo a été revisité pour deux modèles distincts. Le cadre du Dutch Delight de la société Johnny Loco établie à Amsterdam est entièrement en aluminium. Une idée novatrice améliore la sécurité de conduite: l'arrière galbé du cadre est abaissé afin d'éviter le risque de renversement qui existe sur les triporteurs. Avec le Dutch Delight, faire ses courses avec deux enfants ne pose aucun problème. Pour sa part, le beach cruiser associe élégamment la décontraction du design custom californien et la stabilité d'un porte-bagage intégré devant le guidon.

Country: Netherlands · Year: 2007 · Weight: 42 kg · Frame: Steel frame and alloy box · Gears: 3 and 7
Tyres: 24" (front); 26" (rear) · Brakes: Roller brakes

THE VERSATILE
BICYCLE STROLLER

TAGA

The Taga seems so practical, it's a wonder that no one thought of it sooner. In just a few steps and no more than 20 seconds, this Dutch tricycle equipped with gear hub and disc brakes converts to a stroller. The variable aluminum frame can be combined with different features, such as a shopping basket or a second child seat for carrying two offspring at once. A stylish, ecofriendly "mommy taxi" that takes you to—and accompanies you inside—the café.

Das Taga erscheint so praktisch, dass man es eigentlich früher hätte erfinden müssen. Mit wenigen Griffen verwandelt sich das Dreirad aus Holland mit Nabenschaltung und Scheibenbremsen innerhalb von 20 Sekunden in einen Kinderwagen. Der variable Aluminiumrahmen lässt sich mit unterschiedlichen Features wie Einkaufsbox oder Wippe für zwei Kiddies kombinieren. Ein schickes, umweltfreundliches Mama-Taxi, das nach dem Weg zum Café nicht draußen bleiben muss.

Le Taga semble si pratique, que l'on est en droit se demander pourquoi il n'a pas été inventé plus tôt. En deux temps trois mouvements, soit 20 secondes à peine, le petit triporteur hollandais, avec vitesses intégrées au moyeu et freins à disques, se transforme en poussette. Le cadre aluminium multi-positions peut être associé à divers accessoires comme une nacelle pour emmener deux bambins. Une maman-mobile chic et écolo qui passe partout et se gare même dans les restos.

Country: Netherlands · Year: 2009 · Weight: 23 kg · Frame: Aluminum Alloy 6061
Gears: Shimano Nexus 3 · Tyres: 16" · Brakes: Artek Disc Brakes

THE TRUCK ON TWO WHEELS

UMAZOOMA

With 250 watts of power, the umaZooma can transport almost anything. This transporter bike made in Berlin fairly sparkles with appealing details: The spoke lock serves as a parking brake. The transport crate is made of painted birch plywood. With its various covers and weather protection for the child carrier/luggage compartment, the umaZooma is able to brave any weather conditions. The lockable, removable lithium ion battery has a convenient handle, takes only six hours to recharge, and supplies the silent e-motor with almost 19 miles' worth of power.

Mit 250 Watt Unterstützung lässt sich mit dem umaZooma fast alles transportieren. Das Berliner Transportrad glänzt mit liebevollen Details: Das Speichenschloss dient als Standbremse. Die Transportkiste besteht aus lackiertem Birkensperrholz. Verschiedene Abdeckungen und ein Wetter-schutz für den Kinder- oder Kofferraum machen das umaZooma allwettertauglich. Der abschließ- und herausnehmbare Lithium-Ionen-Akku besitzt einen Griff, ist nach sechs Stunden Ladezeit wieder voll einsatzbereit und gibt dem lautlosen E-Motor Power für 30 Kilometer.

Équipé d'un moteur électrique silencieux de 250 watts, l'umaZooma peut transporter presque tout. Ce vélo berlinois présente des détails pratiques, tels que son antivol de cadre qui sert de frein de stationnement. La caisse de transport est en contre-plaqué de bouleau verni. Grâce à divers accessoires et protections, les enfants ou les marchandises embarquées ne craignent pas les intempéries. La batterie lithium-ion amovible est équipée d'un antivol ainsi que d'une poignée de transport. Elle se recharge entièrement en six heures pour une autonomie de 30 km.

Country: Germany · Year: 2011 · Weight: 39 kg · Frame: Steel · Gears: 7 speed Shimano Nexus hub gears
Tyres: 20" (front); 24" (rear) · Brakes: Disc brakes (front); roller brakes (rear)

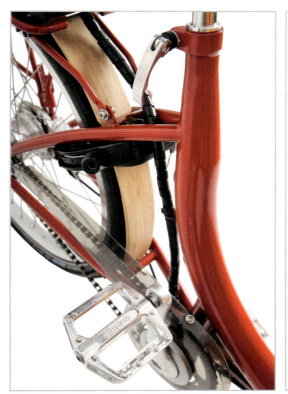

KIDS ROCK

FR8, WORKCYCLES

Two children and an entire week's worth of shopping on one bike? The Fr8 (pronounced "freight") is up to the challenge and its sturdy 4130 CroMoly frame, load carrying geometry and special carriers has a 250 kg capacity. The modular system allows child seats and shopping bags to be distributed both in front and in back, and provides the appropriate integrated footrests. For inseparable twins, there's even the possibility of installing two seats on the rear carrier. The Fr8 does whatever it needs to do without complaint, perfectly in line with company founder Henry Cutler's motto: "Do more with less."

Zwei Kinder und der gesamte Wocheneinkauf auf einem Rad? Das Fr8 (Freight für Last) ist für diese Aufgabe konzipiert. Heavy-Duty-Laufräder mit 13-Gramm-Speichen, stabiler 4130-ChroMoly-Rahmen und der Mittelständer vertragen 250 Kilogramm Zuladung. Das modulare System erlaubt die Verteilung von Kindersitzen und Packtaschen vor und hinter dem Sattel, entsprechende Fußstützen sind integriert. Für unzertrennliche Zwillinge gibt es als Option einen Doppelsitz am Heck. Das Fr8 tut klaglos, was es soll, ganz nach dem Motto des Firmengründers Henry Cutler, das da lautet: „Do more with less."

Deux enfants plus les courses de la semaine sur un vélo? Le Fr8, ou freight (le fret) en langage SMS anglais, est la solution. Bien répartie sur les porte-bagages spéciaux, la charge supportée par le robuste cadre en acier 4130 ChroMoly atteint les 250 kg. Le système modulaire permet de répartir les sièges enfants et les sacoches devant et derrière la selle. Des cale-pieds sont intégrés. Pour les jumeaux inséparables, on peut installer le double siège à l'arrière. Le Fr8 exécute ses tâches sans broncher, fidèle à la devise du fondateur de l'entreprise Henry Cutler: «Do more with less» (faites plus avec moins).

Country: Netherlands · Year: 2008 · Weight: 22–30 kg · Frame: 4130 chromium molybdenum steel · Gears: Shimano Nexus internal gear hub, 8 or 3 speed · Tyres: 26" · Brakes: Shimano Rollerbrakes

E-BIKES

I AM ECLECTRIC

SMART ELECTRIC BIKE, SMART

Even less parking space than their flashy small cars needs the smart electric bike which carries some intelligent new details and solutions. A control unit serving as electronic lock and a dock for a smartphone that functions as navigation center—these are only two of the clever solutions for the smart ebike presented by the car manufacturer. Remove the control unit from the cradle that's integrated into the handlebars and the drive system is deactivated. The smart ebike recovers power from regenerative braking to recharge the battery smoothly integrated as part of the frame and, of course, supplies the smartphone via a USB port with energy while you ride. The specially developed app gives the rider added informations.

Benötigen die Stadtflitzer von smart schon wenig Parkraum, geht der Autohersteller mit seinem electric bike noch einen Schritt weiter in Richtung urbane Mobilität. Die Steuer- und Informations-zentrale als elektronisches Schloss ist nur eine der schlauen Lösungen des flotten Citymobils. Fehlt die Konsole im Dock am Lenker, ist der Antrieb deaktiviert. Beim Bremsen gewinnt das smart ebike Energie zurück, um den im Rahmen integrierten Akku aufzuladen. Ein Smartphone kann als Navigationssystem sicher am Lenker fixiert werden und erhält während der Fahrt über einen USB-Anschluss Energie. Eine eigene App fürs ebike liefert weitere Informationen und Funktionen.

Après les petits bolides smart peu gourmands en espace, le constructeur automobile poursuit l'aventure de la mobilité urbaine avec un vélo électrique. La centrale de commande et d'information qui sert d'antivol électronique n'est que l'une des nombreuses astuces de ce fringant véhicule urbain. Par exemple, sans la console se logeant dans le dock du guidon, l'entraînement est désactivé. Au freinage, le vélo smart récupère de l'énergie afin de recharger les batteries intégrées au cadre. Un smartphone fixé au guidon sert de GPS tout en se rechargeant pendant le trajet grâce à une prise USB. Une application spécialement conçue fournit des informations et des fonctions supplémentaires.

Country: Germany · Year: 2012 · Weight: 26.1 kg · Frame: Aluminium
Gears: Integrated SRAM I-Motion 3 · Tyres: 26 x 1,75" · Brakes: Magura MT4

THE FORMULA 1 CITYBIKE

GOCYCLE G2R, KARBON KINETICS LTD.

When a posh English automotive engineer designs his own bicycle, the result is a futuristic vehicle perfect for Earth's city centers. A clean-running micro-motor, enclosed Cleandrive, and electronic 3-speed gearbox were just as important to Richard Thorpe—who was previously employed by McLaren—as a simple folding mechanism and trouble-free transport on London's tube and bus system. The frame and quick-release interchangable PitstopWheel are made of light-weight injection-molded magnesium, a first for this category.

Entwirft ein englischer Nobelauto-Ingenieur ein eigenes Rad, entsteht ein futuristisches Mobil, perfekt für die Innenstadt der Metropolen dieses Planeten. Sauberer Antrieb durch Micromotor, gekapselter Cleandrive und elektronische 3-Gang-Schaltung waren Richard Thorpe, der für McLaren arbeitete, genauso wichtig wie einfacher Klappmechanismus und problemloser Transport in Londons Tube- und Bus-System. Rahmen und schnell demontierbare PitstopWheel-Laufräder bestehen aus leichtem gegossenem Magnesium, ein Novum für diese Kategorie.

Lorsqu'un ingénieur anglais, spécialiste des voitures de prestige, conçoit son propre vélo, il élabore un véhicule futuriste, idéal pour le centre-ville des métropoles. Pour Richard Thorpe, ancien de chez McLaren, une transmission Cleandrive parfaitement hermétique, associée à un micromoteur et à trois vitesses commandées électroniquement, était aussi importante qu'un mécanisme de pliage simple permettant d'emporter facilement le vélo dans le métro ou les bus londoniens. Le cadre et les roues PitstopWheel rapidement démontables sont en magnésium moulé — une nouveauté dans cette catégorie.

Country: United Kingdom · Year: 2012 · Weight: 15.6 kg · Frame: Injection-moulded magnesium
Gears: Shimano Nexus electronic 3 speed · Tyres: 20" · Brakes: Full hydraulic disc

MOST PRACTICAL

VOLTITUDE, VOLTITUDE S.A.

It looks like a Swiss Army knife and is every bit as practical and universal in its functioning. The Voltitude combines an original design with every-day usability and minimal storage dimensions. When folded, this snazzy Swiss folding bike is only 60 cm wide and 85 cm tall. The low center of gravity, disc brakes, and normal wheelbase carry this red speedster—made of recycled aluminum—quickly and safely through the maze of city traffic.

Sieht aus wie ein Schweizer Taschenmesser, funktioniert auch so praktisch und universell. Das Voltitude kombiniert originelles Design mit Alltags-tauglichkeit und minimalen Staumaßen. Das pfiffige Schweizer Klapprad weist zusammengelegt in Breite und Höhe nur 60 auf 85 Zentimeter auf. Im Stadtverkehr bringen der tiefe Schwerpunkt, die Scheibenbremsen und der normale Radstand den roten Flitzer aus recyceltem Aluminium schnell und sicher durchs Verkehrsgetümmel.

S'il rappelle les célèbres couteaux suisses par son esthétique, il se révèle tout aussi pratique et multifonctions à l'usage. Le Voltitude combine design original, utilisation quotidienne et mensurations minimales: replié, l'astucieux vélo suisse ne mesure que 60 cm sur 85. En circulation, son centre de gravité très bas, ses freins à disques et la position naturelle de conduite, garantissent un trajet des plus sûrs au guidon du petit bolide rouge réalisé en aluminium recyclé.

Country: Switzerland · Year: 2012 · Weight: 25 kg · Frame: Aluminium · Gears: 7 speed in-board hub
Tyres: 12.5" · Brakes: Hydraulic disc brakes

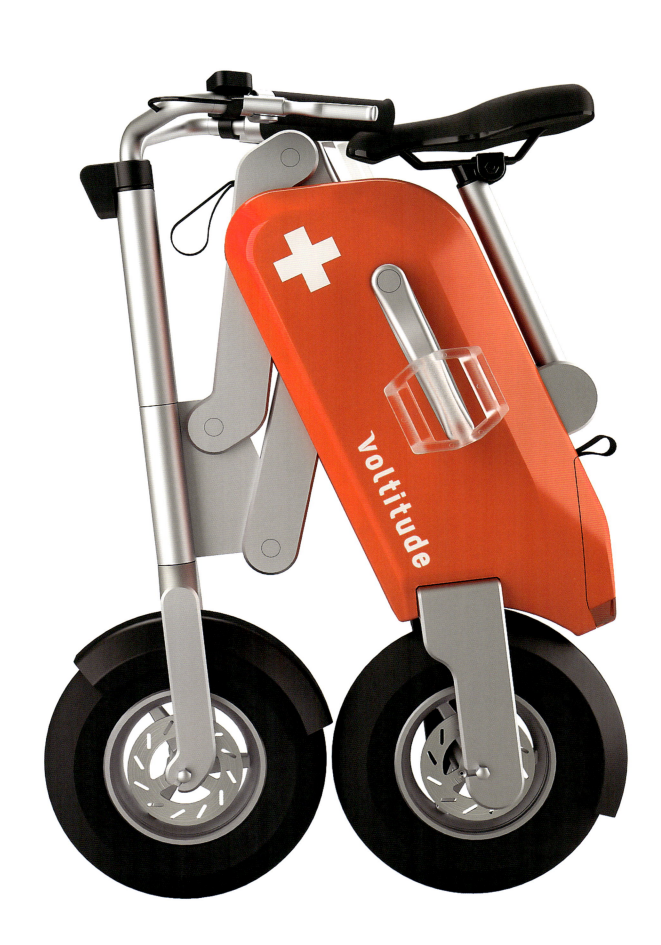

HISTORY WITH A BOOST

DOVER 125TH IMPULSE, RALEIGH UNIVEGA GMBH

This anniversary-edition bicycle from the traditional English manufacturer Raleigh proudly wears the label "Best of Britain" and combines a retro look with state-of-the-art bicycle technology. In addition to its classic design—the men's model comes in British racing green—the Dover uses the latest pedelec technology, including the impulse drive system and progressive power delivery from the central motor. The Retro headlight has a sensor and parking light, and the rear light includes a brake light. The battery is cleverly integrated between the seat post and rear wheel so as not to interfere with the classic lines.

„Best of Britain" steht stolz auf dem deutschen Jubiläumsrad der englischen Traditionsmarke Raleigh. Retro-Look mit modernster Rad-Technik: Neben der klassischen Gestaltung – das Herrenmodell kommt in British Racing Green – weist das Dover modernste Pedelec-Technik auf, wie den Impulse-Antrieb und die progressive Kraftentfaltung des Mittelmotors. Der Retro-Frontscheinwerfer verfügt über Sensor und Standlicht, das Rücklicht beinhaltet Bremsleuchten. Der Akku ist geschickt zwischen Sitzrohr und Hinterrad integriert, um die klassischen Linien nicht zu stören.

«Best of Britain»: le fabricant Raleigh l'affiche fièrement sur son vélo anniversaire qui associe aux dernières techniques un look résolument vieille Angleterre. Sous sa robe classique – le modèle homme arbore une livrée British Racing Green – le Dover est équipé de la dernière technologie Pedelec qui inclut une transmission Impulse et une montée en puissance progressive du moteur central. Le phare rétro placé à l'avant dispose d'un capteur et d'un feu de position, l'éclairage arrière s'allume au freinage. La batterie intelligemment placée entre le tube de selle et la roue arrière ne nuit pas aux lignes de ce vélo classique.

Country: Germany · Year: 2012 · Weight: 24.6 kg · Frame: Aluminium · Gears: Shimano Nexus · Tyres: 28" · Brakes: Magura HS 11

WIRELESS REVOLUTION

SHADOW EBIKE, DAYMAK

What's clever about this bike is what you don't see. The Shadow is the world's first wireless electric bike. Neither gear cables nor brake cables nor electric wires from the motor are visible on this bike from the Canadian company Daymak. The wireless controller operates on its own frequency in the 2.4 GHz range. Magnetic regenerative brakes are installed in front. When you ease up on the throttle, the e-motor builds up negative torque.

Der Clou an diesem E-Bike ist unsichtbar. Das Shadow ist das weltweit erste kabellose Elektrobike. Weder Schaltzüge noch Bremskabel oder elektrische Leitungen am Motor sind am Rad der kanadischen Firma Daymak zu finden. Die drahtlose Kontrolleinheit arbeitet auf einer eigenen Frequenz im 2,4-GHz-Bereich. Die Vorderbremse funktioniert regenerativ über Magneten. Nimmt man „Gas" zurück, wird über den E-Motor ein negativ gerichtetes Drehmoment aufgebaut.

La spécificité de ce vélo électrique est invisible: le Shadow est le premier modèle sans fil au monde. Ce produit de l'entreprise canadienne Daymak ne présente ni câbles de frein, ni levier de vitesse, ni fils électriques reliés au moteur. L'unité de contrôle sans fil fonctionne avec sa propre fréquence de 2,4 GHz. La roue avant intègre un système magnétique de récupération d'énergie au freinage. Quand on «coupe les gaz», le moteur électrique génère un couple négatif.

Country: Canada · Year: 2011 · Weight: 28 kg · Frame: Aluminum · Gears: Singlespeed · Tyres: 26" · Brakes: Wireless brakes

THE NO-NONSENSE PEDELEC

CELL CITY, MY-E-BIKE.COM

The Cell City from the German vendor my-e-bike.com boasts a clear design idiom. The end-to-end dynamic aluminium main frame tube gives the Cell City a very neat look. The e-motor is concealed in the front hub. The hydraulic disc brakes have a motor-assisted interruption safety system (MUSS) that effectively supports riding safety. The pedal-assisted drive offers 250 watts of power and the lithium ion battery has a range of over 40 miles.

Das Cell City des deutschen Versenders my-e-bike.com spricht eine klare Formensprache. Das durchgängige dynamische Hauptrahmen-Rohr aus Aluminium lässt das Cell City sehr aufgeräumt wirken. Der E-Motor versteckt sich in der Vordernabe. Die hydraulischen Scheibenbremsen besitzen ein Motorschub-Unterbrechungs-Sicherheits-System, genannt MUSS, das wirksam zur Fahrsicherheit beiträgt. Der „pedal assisted"-Antrieb leistet 250 Watt und ermöglicht mit dem Lithium-Ionen-Akku eine Reichweite bis zu 65 Kilometer.

Le Cell City de l'expéditeur allemand my-e-bike.com affiche clairement sa philosophie. Son cadre formé d'un bout à l'autre par une poutre centrale en aluminium témoigne d'un certain sens de l'ordre. Le moteur électrique se loge dans le moyeu avant. Les freins à disques hydrauliques sont équipés d'un système d'interruption du moteur appelé MUSS qui contribue efficacement à la sécurité de conduite. L'entraînement «pedal assisted» délivre 250 watts, alors que les batteries lithium-ion offrent une autonomie allant jusqu'à 65 km.

Country: Germany · Year: 2011 · Weight: 21.8 kg · Frame: Aluminium · Gears: Shimano Nexus 3 Speed inner gear · Tyres: 26" · Brakes: Shimano hydraulic disc brakes

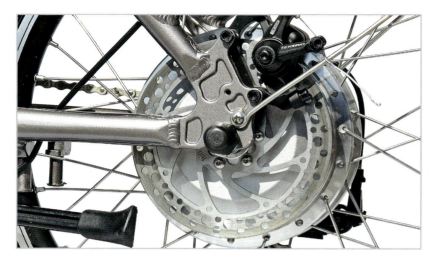

JUICED UP

ODK U500 E-BIKE, JUICED RIDERS INC.

Tora Harris, the young American founder of Juiced Riders Inc., was looking for efficient transportation solutions. What he found was a combination e-bike and cargo bike. The solid aluminum frame with integrated cargo rack is made in China, and while its components are nothing very special, they're extremely reliable. That's because the goal of the ODK U500 wasn't just sustainability but also affordability, plus a fresh and sassy look. A battery with twice the usual capacity guarantees a long range.

Tora Harris, der junge amerikanische Gründer von Juiced Riders Inc., war auf der Suche nach effizienten Transportlösungen und fand die Antwort in der Kombination aus E-Bike und Cargo-Rad. Der solide Aluminiumrahmen mit integrierter Gepäckbasis ist made in China und trägt keine außergewöhnlichen, aber extrem zuverlässige Komponenten. Denn neben Haltbarkeit war ein erschwinglicher Preis das Ziel für das ODK U500, das in frischem, frechem Look auftritt. Ein Akku mit doppelt so hoher Kapazität wie üblich garantiert eine große Reichweite.

L'Américain Tora Harris, jeune fondateur de Juiced Riders Inc., cherchait un moyen de transport efficace. Il a trouvé la réponse en combinant un vélo électrique et un vélo de transport. Le solide cadre en aluminium avec porte-bagage intégré est made in China. Son équipement ne présente certes rien d'extraordinaire, mais fait preuve d'une extrême fiabilité. Outre la résistance, l'objectif de l'ODK U500 était de proposer, à un prix abordable, un vélo au look frais, voire insolent. Une batterie d'une capacité deux fois plus importante que la moyenne garantit une grande autonomie.

Country: China · Year: 2011 · Weight: 31.5 kg · Frame: 6061 Aluminum · Gears: 7 speed · Tyres: 20" · Brakes: Tektro Novella disc brake

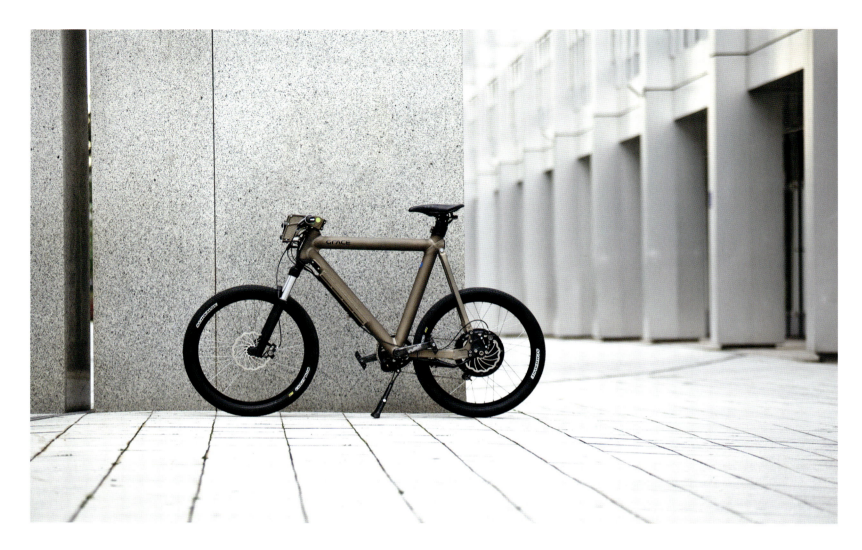

CATCH ME IF YOU CAN

GRACE SERIES, GRACE

The imposing Pro Race frame is built only to-order in the shop of famous German frame- and bike-builder Karl-Heinz Nicolai. Grace bikes are the impressive result of a collaboration between Nicolai and designer Michael Hecken. The Pro Race, which can attain a speed of up to 45 km/h, has a lossless, brushless motor mounted directly on the rear axle. The front headlights are particularly striking, housed in a machined block of aluminum that also contains the information display for the battery, which is seamlessly integrated into the bottom tube.

Der Rahmen des dominanten Pro Race wird nur auf Bestellung in der renommierten Schmiede des deutschen Rahmen- und Bikebauers Karl-Heinz Nicolai produziert. Die Bikes von Grace sind das imposante Ergebnis der Zusammenarbeit von Nicolai mit Designer Michael Hecken. Im bis zu 45 Stundenkilometer schnellen Pro Race arbeitet ein verlustfreier bürstenloser Motor direkt an der Hinterradnabe. Blickfang sind die aus einem Alublock gefrästen Frontscheinwerfer, gleichzeitig Träger des Informationsdisplays für den nahtlos im Rahmenunterrohr integrierten Akku.

Le cadre de cet intimidant Pro Race n'est produit que sur commande dans l'atelier du célèbre fabricant allemand Karl-Heinz Nicolai. Les vélos Grace sont le résultat de la collaboration de ce dernier avec le designer Michael Hecken. Le Pro Race est équipé d'un moteur sans balais, entraînant directement et sans perte de puissance la roue arrière, jusqu'à une vitesse de 45 km/h. Le bloc d'aluminium fraisé, qui sert de logement aux feux avant et de support à l'écran d'affichage de la batterie parfaitement intégrée dans le tube inférieur du cadre, fera inévitablement des envieux.

Country: Germany · Year: 2009 · Weight: 33 kg · Frame: Aluminium · Gears: SRAM X-9 Speed / SRAM X-0 (optional)
Tyres: Schwalbe Crazy Bob 26" · Brakes: Magura Louise 203 mm

MY NAME IS BIKE. EBIKE.

RACE R001, EBIKE

Hightech, stylish and classy—and licensed for fun. The marketing campaign for the young German company EBIKE deliberately quotes the well-known presentation of the most popular British spy of all time. Wolfgang Momberger and Helge von Fugler worked together with engineers, designers and marketing specialists from USA, Asia and Europe to develop the EBIKE brand along with different bike models. The flashy sports model RACE R001, painted orange and red, comes in an aesthetically distinctive style, and the lithium-ion-battery is invisible, integrated in the down tube. The motor in the rear hub delivers 500 watts of power allowing the R001 to accelerate up to 45 km/h. The adjustable front suspension and strong disc brakes ensure that riding is comfortable and safe.

Hightech, Stil und Klasse, mit der Lizenz für Spaß. Marketing und Kampagne für die junge deutsche Firma EBIKE wurden in Anlehnung an den berühmten britischen Agenten gelauncht. Wolfgang Momberger und Helge von Fugler haben mit Ingenieuren, Designern und Marketingexperten aus den USA, Asien und Europa die Marke EBIKE und deren Modelle entwickelt. Das sportliche Modell RACE R001 setzt auf eine schlüssige Formensprache. Der unauffällig im Unterrohr integrierte Lithium-Ionen-Akku powert den Heckmotor mit 500 Watt und bringt den orangefarbenen Flitzer mit den roten Farbakzenten auf bis zu 45 Stundenkilometer. Die einstellbare Federgabel und die großzügig dimensionierten Scheibenbremsen sorgen für Komfort und Fahrsicherheit.

Le hightech, le style, la classe... et le permis de s'amuser en prime. En matière de commercialisation, la jeune entreprise allemande E-Bike a choisi de faire référence au plus célèbre des agents britanniques. Afin de lancer la marque EBIKE et ses modèles, Wolfgang Momberger et Helge von Fugler ont fait appel à des ingénieurs, à des designers et à des spécialistes du marketing venus des États-Unis, d'Asie et d'Europe. Le plus sport, le RACE R001, mise sur une ligne sans compromis. La batterie lithium-ion, discrètement intégrée dans la barre oblique, fournit au moteur installé sur la roue arrière les 500 watts dont il a besoin pour emmener cette furie orange et rouge jusqu'à 45 km/h. La fourche réglable et les freins à disques surdimensionnés sont autant de garanties de confort que de sécurité.

Country: Germany · Year: 2012 · Weight: 25 kg · Frame: Premium aluminium
Gears: 27 · Tyres: 47 mm x 26" · Brakes: Disc Brake, 180/160 mm

WORLD E-CHAMPION

ESPIRE, THIRD ELEMENT

The young Munich-based company Third Element integrates state-of-the-art technology into its e-bikes, including the eSpire. This bike's 1200 watt Clean Mobile motor achieves 90 percent efficiency, enabling it to conquer even steep ascents. The eSpire's frame and swing arm are constructed of extremely rigid tubular aluminum produced by a specialist company. The Magura disc brakes and Rohloff 14-speed gear hub are also based on the most advanced technology. The eSpire was the first official winner of the e-bike world championships.

Modernste Technik verbaut die junge Münchner Firma Third Element in ihren E-Bikes wie dem eSpire. 90 Prozent Effizienz erreicht der Motor von Clean Mobile, der 1200 Watt leistet. Damit lassen sich auch extreme Steigungen bewältigen. Rahmen und Schwinge des eSpire sind in hochsteifer Gitterrohrtechnik in Aluminium ausgeführt, von einer Spezialfirma produziert. Feinste Technik steckt auch in den Magura-Scheibenbremsen und der Rohloff-Nabenschaltung mit 14 Gängen. Das eSpire gewann die erste offizielle E-Bike-Weltmeisterschaft.

La jeune entreprise munichoise intègre les dernières innovations dans ses vélos électriques. Dans l'eSpire, le moteur de 1200 watts conçu par Clean Mobile atteint une efficience de 90 %. Aucune côte ne lui résiste. Le cadre et le bras oscillant réalisés par une entreprise spécialisée adoptent une structure treillis tubulaire en aluminium d'une grande rigidité. Les freins à disques Magura et le moyeu Rohloff à 14 vitesses intégrées témoignent également d'une technique de pointe. L'eSpire a d'ailleurs remporté le premier championnat du monde officiel de vélos électriques.

Country: Germany · Year: 2010 · Weight: 30 kg · Frame: Aluminium · Gears: Rohloff Speedhub with 14 gears · Tyres: 24"
Brakes: Magura hydraulic disc brakes with motor cut off switch

FAST AS LIGHTNING

STEALTH BOMBER, STEALTH ELECTRIC BIKES

The Stealth Bomber looks like a downhill bike on steroids. Extra-long suspension travel and disc brakes emphasize the extreme character of this powerful electric bike. With his Stealth e-bikes, company founder John Karambalis goes beyond conventional bike classes. The weight of the hub motor in the rear wheel improves this downhill bike's traction even more. In competition mode, the Bomber's brushless e-motor manages up to 4,500 watts and with the aid of a 9-speed transmission, pushes the 53-kilogram bike to a maximum speed of 80 kilometers per hour.

Das Stealth Bomber wirkt wie ein Downhill-Bike auf Steroiden. Immense Federwege und Scheiben-bremsen unterstreichen den extremen Charakter des kraftvollen Elektro-Bikes. Firmengründer John Karambalis sieht sich mit seinen Stealth-E-Bikes außerhalb herkömmlicher Bike-Klassen. Der Nabenmotor im Hinterrad verbessert durch sein Gewicht noch die Traktion im Downhill. Der bürstenlose E-Motor des Bombers leitet im Competition Mode bis zu 4 500 Watt und treibt das 53-Kilo-Bike über ein 9-Gang-Getriebe zu einer Höchstgeschwindigkeit von 80 Stundenkilometern.

L'entreprise Stealth, fondée par John Karambalis, fabrique des vélos résolument atypiques. Le Stealth Bomber fait l'effet d'un vélo de descente dopé aux stéroïdes. L'immense débattement des suspensions et les freins à disques témoignent du tempérament extrême que réserve cette véritable bombe électrique. Le moteur sans balais à 9 rapports du moyeu arrière délivre jusqu'à 4 500 watts en mode compétition et emmène les 53 kg du vélo à une vitesse maximale de 80 km/h, l'inertie créée par son poids, augmentant encore la vitesse en descente.

Country: Australia · Year: 2012 · Weight: 53 kg · Frame: CrMo alloys
Gears: 9 speed · Tyres: 24 x 3" · Brakes: 6 Piston

MY FAT GERMAN E-BIKE

BLACKBLOCK DARK CUSTOM, PG

Stars like Lady Gaga and Orlando Bloom ride showpieces from the Regensburg company PG. Run by the young Manuel Ostner, this company is uncompromising in its use of hightech to satisfy its customers' individual desires. The powerful Blackblock with its Clean Mobile drive can be ordered as a pedelec, an e-bike, or a speed pedelec with the potential to reach up to 45 km/h. The solid battery case positioned centrally on the cruiser frame functions as a stylistic element, while the Magura Julie hydraulic disc brakes serve to hold the Blackblock in check.

Stars wie Lady Gaga und Orlando Bloom fahren auf die Showstücke der Regensburger Firma PG ab. Die Company um Jungunternehmer Manuel Ostner setzt kompromisslos Hightech um, so individuell, wie ihre Kunden es wünschen. Das wuchtige Blackblock mit dem Antrieb von Clean Mobile lässt sich als Pedelec, E-Bike oder Kleinkraftrad mit Potenzial bis zu 45 Stundenkilometern ordern. Die massive Akku-Box fungiert als Stilelement, zentral im Cruiser-Rahmen platziert, packende Magura-Julie-Hydraulikbremsen sollen das Blackblock im Zaum halten.

Des stars comme Lady Gaga ou Orlando Bloom aiment rouler sur les mécaniques sans compromis de PG. L'entreprise de Regensburg du jeune Manuel Ostner réalise des créations hightech en fonction des souhaits de chacun de ses clients. L'imposant Blackblock, qui utilise une transmission de Clean Mobile, peut être commandé en version Pedelec, vélo électrique ou cyclomoteur avec un potentiel de 45 km/h. L'imposant boîtier de batterie vient orner un cadre typé personnalisé. Les freins à disque hydraulique Magura Julie ne sont pas de trop pour maîtriser le Blackblock.

Country: Germany · Year: 2011 · Weight: 39 kg · Frame: Steel – handmade in Germany
Gears: SRAM-P5 (5 gear shift) · Tyres: Schwalbe Crazy Bob, 26" · Brakes: Magura Julie Hydraulic Disc brakes

ACCESSORIES

BELOWFOUR CASE
ILYA FRIDMAN

This unique picnic basket perches on the seat post. Australian designer Ilya Fridman created this robust plastic egg whose fastener also serves as a built-in handle.

Die Picknickbox an der Sattelstütze. Der australische Designer Ilya Fridman entwarf das stabile Kunststoff-Ei, dessen Befestigung als integrierter Henkel genutzt wird.

Le panier pique-nique fixé à la tige de selle. Le designer australien Ilya Fridman a créé cet œuf en plastique remarquable de stabilité, dont la fixation sert de poignée intégrée.

HANDLEBAR BOTTLE BAG
PASHLEY

So very British! The hand-sewn aniline leather and reinforced ends of the Handlebar Bottle Bag ensure a safe passage for a bottle of single malt or a copy of the "Times."

Very british. Handgenähtes Anilin-Leder und verstärkte Abschlüsse der Handlebar Bottle Bag sorgen für einen sicheren Transport der Single-Malt-Flasche oder der „Times".

So british. La bouteille de single malt et le «Times» sont en parfaite sécurité dans cette sacoche de guidon en cuir aniline cousue main avec boucles renforcées.

THE ORIGINAL LEATHER FRAME BAG FROM LEIPZIG
RETROVELO

This bag made of heavy-duty leather has two compartments suitable for a laptop, documents and breakfast. The fastener around the top tube is as sturdy as it is simple. The Frame Bag also lets you avoid the clammy back that comes from wearing a backpack.

Die Retrovelo-Rahmentasche aus kräftigem Leder nimmt in zwei Abteilen Laptop, Unterlagen und Frühstück auf. Die Befestigung am Oberrohr ist gleichermaßen simpel wie stabil und erspart den feuchten Rücken eines Rucksacktransports.

Ce porte-document Retrovelo en cuir épais permet de ranger dans deux compartiments un portable, un petit déjeuner et des dossiers. Simple et sûre, la fixation sur la barre horizontale du cadre supprime l'inévitable problème de transpiration lié aux sacs à dos.

6PACK BAG
DONKEY PRODUCTS

Donkey, the Designlabel from Hamburg creates urban gifts, or extraordinary objects for everyday use, including this 6pack for bike frames. The reinforced, zippered canvas bag holds up to three liters.

Donkey, das Designlabel aus Hamburg, kreiert Urban Gifts und außergewöhnliche Dinge für den Alltag wie den 6pack für den Fahrradrahmen. Die verstärkte Canvastasche mit Klettsicherung transportiert drei Liter.

Donkey crée à Hambourg toutes sortes de choses pratiques au quotidien comme le 6pack pour cadre de vélo. Le casier en toile renforcée, équipé de velcros, supporte jusqu'à 6 bouteilles de 50 cl.

CAPS IN STYLE
HELT-PRO

Cap or hat, but always a head protection. The German company helt-pro turns every head protection into a personal statement.

Mütze, Kappe oder Hut, aber immer ein Kopfschutz. Mit der deutschen Firma helt-pro wird jeder Fahrrad-Kopfschutz zum persönlichen Statement.

Bonnet, casquette ou chapeau, mais bel et bien un protection de la tête. La société allemande helt-pro permet à ses clients d'exprimer leur personnalité au moyen de leur protection de la tête.

I LOVE MY BRAIN
NUTCASE

Safety doesn't have to be boring. Designer Michael Morrow of Portland thought bike helmets were unimaginative, so he created his own brand of unique multisport helmets.

Sicherheit muss nicht langweilig sein. Designer Michael Morrow aus Portland fand Radhelme uninspiriert und gründete eine eigene Marke, die unverwechselbare Multisporthelme produziert.

Sécurité ne doit pas rimer avec morosité. Michael Morrow, un designer de Portland qui trouvait les casques ennuyeux, a fondé sa propre société afin de produire des casques multisports uniques en leur genre.

SMART ONE & SMART TWO
YAKKAY

YAKKAY supplies interchangeable covers for its own helmets so that you can match your style covering to your mood or to the weather.

YAKKAY liefert zum eigenen Helm wechselbare Überzüge, sodass man, je nach Wetter und Laune, optisch unterschiedlich behütet losfahren kann.

Pour chaque casque, YAKKAY propose plusieurs housses interchangeables, si bien qu'il est possible d'adapter l'aspect de son couvre-chef à la météo ou à son envie.

LEGGITS – RAIN OVERSHOES
GEORGIA IN DUBLIN

The mother-daughter team of Nicola Orriss and Georgia Scott combines a love of design with a passion for biking. Leggits protect the fashionable woman's shoes from rain and mud. The soles are made from recycled bike inner tubes.

Mutter und Tochter, Nicola Orriss und Georgia Scott, verbindet ihre Liebe zu Design und Radfahren. Die Leggits schonen schicke Frauenschuhe bei Regen und Matsch, die Sohlen bestehen aus recycelten Fahrradschläuchen.

Nicola Orriss et sa fille Georgia Scott partagent le même amour du design et du vélo. Leurs élégantes surchaussures protègent les chaussures de la boue et de la pluie. Les semelles sont faites à partir de chambres à air recyclées.

RAINWRAP
GEORGIA IN DUBLIN

Quick and easy to put on—and even usable as a picnic blanket—the Rainwrap rain and wind protector with a safety reflector on the back is both simple and ingenious.

Schnell umgewickelt und sogar als Picknickdecke nutzbar. Der Regen- und Windschutz Rainwrap mit Sicherheitsreflektor auf der Rückseite ist einfach und genial.

Vite enfilée, la Rainwrap protège de la pluie et du vent. Cette jupe, à la fois simple et géniale, est équipée de réflecteurs à l'arrière. Elle se révèle aussi utile lors des pique-niques.

ORATORY JACKET
BROMPTON BICYCLE LTD.

Waterproof siliconized cotton, reflectors on the underside of the collar, and a pull-out, hi-viz rear panel for visibility in the dark: the Oratory Jacket has lots of clever detailing for the urban biker.

Silikonisierte Baumwolle gegen Regen, Reflektoren unterm Kragen, ausklappbarer Regenschutz im unteren Rücken: Das Oratory Jacket steckt voller ausgeklügelter Details für den urbanen Radfahrer.

Le coton siliconé pour se protéger de la pluie, des réflecteurs sous le col et une protection pluie escamotable sur le bas du dos: cette veste renferme de nombreuses astuces pour tout cycliste urbain.

SPECIAL & CONCEPT BIKES

SCANDINAVIAN BEAUTY

DV01, DAVID QVICK

The DV01 is David Qvick's attempt to achieve the perfect combination of aesthetics and function. According to this young Swedish product designer from Falun—a graduate of the University of Gothenburg's renowned HDK School of Design and Crafts—a bike must not only fulfill its transportation function, but must also express the personal style of its owner. The clear, understated appearance of this single-speed bike is emphasized even more by the internal cable routing and the minimalist design of the wooden handlebars and cargo rack.

Die perfekte Kombination aus Ästhetik und Funktion will David Qvick mit seinem DV01 realisieren. Ein Fahrrad sollte neben seiner Transportfunktion unbedingt den persönlichen Stil seines Besitzers ausdrücken, so der junge schwedische Produktdesigner aus Falun, der an der renommierten Göteborger Hochschule für Design und Kunsthandwerk HDK studierte. Die zurückgenommene, klare Optik des Singlespeed-Bikes wird durch die innen verlegten Züge und die minimalistische Ausführung des Lenkers und Gepäckträgers aus Holz noch unterstrichen.

David Qvick, ancien étudiant de la célèbre école de design et d'artisanat d'art HDK de Göteborg, voulait réaliser avec son DV01 l'union parfaite de l'utile et de l'esthétique. Outre sa fonction de transport, un vélo devrait toujours représenter le style personnel de son propriétaire. C'est en tout cas l'avis du concepteur de produits suédois désormais installé à Falun. Les lignes claires et l'aspect dépouillé de ce vélo à une seule vitesse sont soulignés par le passage des câbles dans le cadre et l'aspect minimaliste du guidon et du porte-bagage en bois.

Country: Sweden · Year: 2011 · Weight: 9.5 kg · Frame: Columbus Chromoly steel tubing
Gears: single speed · Tyres: 28" · Brakes: Tektro R559 (long arms)

SOLID ELEGANCE

B2O-VÉLO-BAMBOU, FRITSCH DURISOTTI

French designers Antoine Fritsch and Vivien Durisotti have built a highly streamlined bike using their favorite material: bamboo. The most complex component of the B2o-vélo-bambou is its gear hub. The frame consists of only a main carrier and doesn't even have a headset. The handlebars are integrated using steel plates. The seat's pillow design is also far from traditional. Only 50 bikes will roll out of this design studio on the banks of the Seine.

Die französischen Designer Antoine Fritsch und Vivien Durisotti bauten ein extrem reduziertes Bike aus ihrem Lieblingsmaterial, aus Bambusholz. Das komplexeste Teil am B2o-vélo-bambou ist die Nabenschaltung. Der Rahmen besteht lediglich aus einem Hauptträger, selbst auf einen Steuersatz wird verzichtet und die Lenkung über Stahlplatten integriert. Auch der Sattel ist durch seine Kissenform weit von herkömmlichen Designs entfernt. Lediglich 50 Exemplare verließen das Studio am Seine-Ufer.

Les designers français Antoine Fritsch et Vivien Durisotti ont conçu un vélo extrêmement minimaliste dans leur matériau favori: le bambou. Le composant le plus complexe du B2o-vélo-bambou est le moyeu à vitesses intégrées. Le cadre est constitué d'une poutre centrale. Les deux créateurs sont allés jusqu'à remplacer la direction traditionelle par une simple charnière. La selle, qui ressemble à un coussin, se démarque aussi des formes habituelles. Seuls 50 exemplaires ont quitté l'atelier des bords de Seine.

Country: France · Year: 2006 · Weight: 12 kg · Frame: Natural bamboo · Gears: 7 · Tyres: 26" · Brakes: Retro braking

DEEP IN THE WOODS

WOODWAY, ARNDT MENKE

Form meets function. The Woodway is constructed from pine tubes—probably the lightest and most stable form this wood can take. The fibers are lattice-wound to increase stability. Consequently, the Woodway design project frame by Arndt Menke weighs a mere 2.3 kilograms. Laminated ash-wood seat stays provide a cushioning effect. The look and feel of this aesthetically pleasing road bike frame is inspired by wooden sports equipment, such as hockey sticks and tennis rackets.

Form trifft auf Funktion: Das Woodway besteht aus Kiefernrohren, der wohl leichtesten und gleichzeitig stabilsten Art, Holz zu verarbeiten. Die Holzfaser ist dabei kreuzweise angeordnet. So bringt der Designprojekt-Rahmen Woodway von Arndt Menke ein Gewicht von nur 2,3 Kilogramm auf die Waage. Dämpfende Funktion üben laminierte Eschenholzfedern als Sitzstreben aus. Look and Feel dieses ästhetischen Roadbike-Rahmens sind an klassische, aus Holz gefertigte Sportgeräte wie Hockey- oder Tennisschläger angelehnt.

Le design et le fonctionnel réunis. Le designer Arndt Menke a choisi pour son projet Woodway de faire appel à des tubes de pin ainsi qu'à des fibres tressées et renforcées. Usiné sous forme de tubes, le pin se présente sous sa forme à la fois la plus légère et la plus stable qui soient. Le cadre ne pèse que 2.3 kg. Les haubans absorbent les chocs grâce à des ressorts en bois de frêne laminé. L'esthétique de ce cadre et les sensations que procure ce vélo de route sont directement inspirées d'anciens instruments sportifs en bois tels que les crosses et les raquettes.

Country: Germany · Year: 2008 · Weight: 2.3 kg · Frame: Pine and ash · Gears: Singlespeed · Tyres: 28"

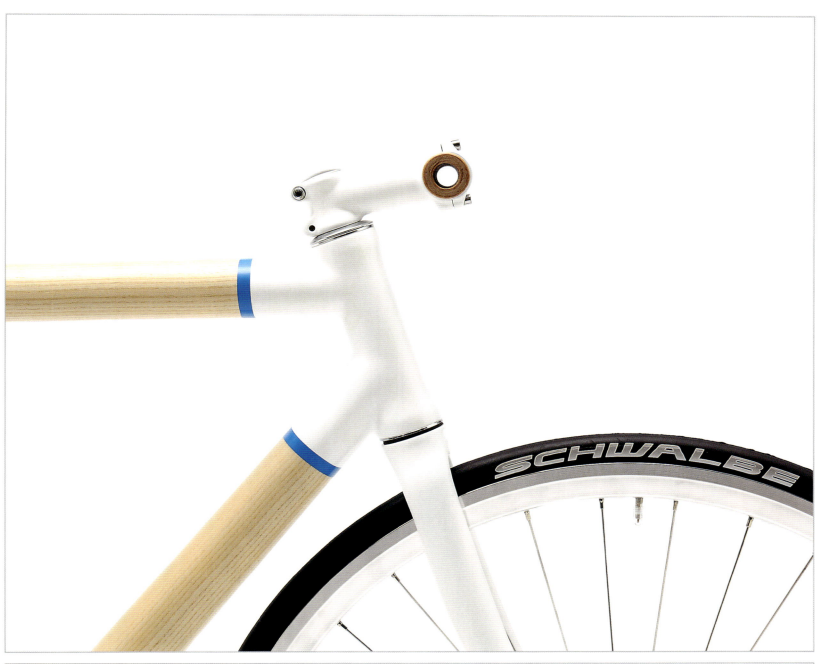

INNER VALUES

CARBONWOOD BICYCLE, GARY GALEGO

With his Carbonwood, Gary Galego has created a one-of-a-kind combination: carbon is sandwiched between layers of plywood to reinforce the frame. Every bike is hand-built in Sydney. The individually selected wood makes each Carbonwood a visually unique creation. The Australian interior designer Galego is fascinated by the dual role of bicycles as sports equipment and transportation. His passion for detail in craftsmanship is what makes the Carbonwood a flawless work of art with a spirit all its own.

Gary Galego kreiert mit dem Carbonwood eine einzigartige Verbindung: Carbon zwischen den Lagen des Schichtholzes verstärkt den Rahmen. Jedes Rad entsteht ausschließlich in Handarbeit in Sydney. Durch die individuelle Auswahl des verwendeten Holzes wird jedes Carbonwood optisch zum Unikat. Den australischen Interior-Designer fasziniert die Doppelrolle des Rads als Sportgerät und Transportmittel. Seine Liebe zum Detail in der Verarbeitung macht das Carbonwood zu einem makellosen Kunstwerk mit eigener Seele.

Gary Galego a réussi une association exceptionnelle avec le Carbonwood : le carbone vient s'intercaler entre les lames de bois pour renforcer le cadre. Chaque vélo est produit artisanalement dans un atelier de Sydney et arbore une robe unique étant donné le caractère tout aussi unique du bois sélectionné. L'architecte d'intérieur australien est fasciné par la double fonction du vélo: à la fois mode de déplacement et pratique sportive. Son amour du détail, observable à tout moment de la fabrication, donne véritablement une âme à chacune de ces authentiques œuvres d'art.

Country: Australia · Year: 2009 · Weight: 10 kg · Frame: Carbon fibre, plywood, wood, chromoly steel seat tube and bottom bracket · Gears: fixed gear, chain ring 40 teeth / rear sprocket 15 teeth · Tyres: 28" · Brakes: Front hydraulic disc

OUT OF AFRICA

SINGLESPEED, BAMBOORIDE

The Singlespeed's frame is handmade in Ghana by Ibrahim Nyampong and his team. The lightweight bike is then assembled by the Austrian company Bambooride using simple, sustainable components that don't detract from the natural look. Because bamboo is an extremely durable material, even harsh city traffic won't damage this natural bike. The mature fiber composite material is naturally lightweight. The frame weighs about the same as its aluminum equivalent with the same bending stiffness.

Der Rahmen des Singlespeed wird in Ghana von Ibrahim Nyampong und einem Team handgefertigt, die österreichische Schmiede Bambooride komplettiert das Leichtbau-Rad mit einfachen, haltbaren Komponenten, die nicht vom natürlichen Look ablenken sollen. Bambus ist ein extrem stabiler Werkstoff, sodass auch der harte Stadtverkehr dem Naturrad nicht schadet. Er ist ein gewachsener Faserverbundstoff und somit ein natürliches Leichtbaumaterial. Der Rahmen ist bei gleicher Biegesteifigkeit etwa so schwer wie ein Pendant aus Aluminium.

Le cadre du Singlespeed est réalisé à la main au Ghana par Ibrahim Nyampong et son équipe. L'atelier autritian Bambooride complète la structure légère d'éléments simples et durables, correspondant au look naturel du vélo. Le bambou présente une pellicule supérieure extrêmement résistante, si bien que la pollution urbaine n'affecte pas ce vélo naturel. Véritable fibre composite organique, il constitue un matériau de construction à la fois léger et organique. Pour une résistance à la flexion égale, le cadre pèse aussi peu que son équivalent en aluminium.

Country: Austria · Year: 2012 · Weight: 8.5 kg · Frame: Bamboo · Tyres: 28" · Brakes: XLC Comp Road-Brake BR-R01

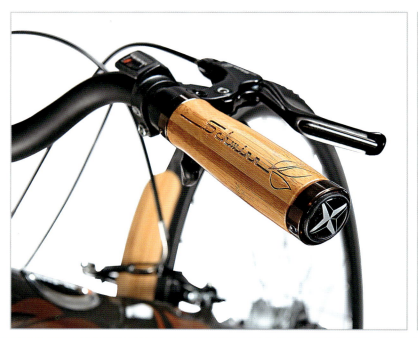

SHINING EXAMPLE

VESTIGE BIKE, SCHWINN

To create the most eco-friendly urban bike of all time, Schwinn builds its Vestige frame out of flax fibers. These fibers are as light and sturdy as carbon but are biodegradable. Schwinn takes advantage of another of this material's properties: its translucence. Internal LEDs make the Vestige glow in the dark, while a hub dynamo supplies the necessary power. Other eco-components include bamboo fenders and grips, tires made of recyclable rubber, and water-soluble paint.

Das umweltfreundlichste Urban-Bike aller Zeiten. Beim Vestige-Rahmen setzt Schwinn auf Flachsfasern. Diese sind so leicht und stabil wie Carbon, jedoch biologisch abbaubar. Schwinn nutzt eine weitere Eigenschaft des Materials: Licht kann die Fasern passieren und so leuchtet das Vestige durch integrierte LEDs auffällig im Dunkeln. Ein Nabendynamo produziert die nötige Spannung. Weitere Bio-Komponenten: Schutzbleche und Griffe bestehen aus Bambus, die Reifen aus recycelbarem Gummi, die Lackierung aus einem Lack auf Wasserbasis.

Le vélo urbain le plus respectueux de l'environnement jamais construit. Pour le cadre, Schwinn a choisi la fibre de lin: un matériau aussi léger et stable que le carbone, mais biologique et, surtout, translucide. Le Vestige tire parti de cette caractéristique pour s'illuminer dans la pénombre grâce à des LED intégrées. L'énergie nécessaire est produite par une dynamo intégrée au moyeu. Le vélo fait appel à d'autres composants d'origine végétale: le garde-boue et les poignées en bambou, les pneus en gomme recyclable et la peinture en phase aqueuse.

Country: USA · Year: 2012 · Frame: Flax fiber · Gears: 9 speed · Tyres: 26" · Brakes: Schwinn Alloy V-Brake

LIKE NO OTHER

BESPOKE COLLECTION, DERRINGER CYCLES

Derringer Cycles' Bespoke Collection includes customized bikes only. Designed by Adrian Van Anz, every Derringer Cycle that leaves the workshop is one of a kind. These bikes were inspired by 1920's board track racers. A 4-stroke engine displacing 50 ccm propels the bike while the pedal drive is decoupled. Every Derringer is hand-built in Los Angeles to suit the customer's exact preferences.

Derringer Cycles bieten in ihrer Bespoke Collection nur Maßgeschneidertes. Kein Derringer Cycle, gestaltet von Designer Adrian Van Anz, das die Werkstatt verlässt, gleicht dem anderen. Die Bikes sind Reminiszenzen an Rennen, die in den 20er Jahren auf holzbeplankten Bahnovalen ausgetragen wurden. Ein Viertaktmotor mit 50 Kubikzentimeter treibt die Bikes an, der Pedalantrieb wird über eine Kupplung dabei entkoppelt. Jedes Derringer entsteht in Los Angeles in Handarbeit nach Kundenwünschen.

Derringer Cycles ne propose que du taillé sur mesure dans sa collection Bespoke. Chaque vélo Derringer qui sort de l'atelier du designer Adrian Van Anz est différent des autres. Ils se font l'écho des courses des années 1920, qui avaient lieu sur des pistes ovales recouvertes de plancher. Ils sont animés par un moteur quatre temps 50 cm. Les mouvements du pédalier sont découplés par un embrayage. Chaque Derringer est produit artisanalement à Los Angeles selon les souhaits du client.

Country: USA · Year: 2011 · Weight: 34 kg · Frame: Steel · Tyres: 26" · Brakes: Drum brakes

YOU NAME IT

WRITE A BIKE, JURI ZAECH

This is a playful use of lettering and design, and a project with no pretensions to feasibility. The Write-a-Bike—conceived by Swiss designer and typographer Juri Zaech who resides in Paris—is remarkable for its lightness and the organic combination of lettering and hardware that is the bike frame. At first glance, the designs look functional and three-dimensional. Only a closer examination reveals that the bikes are purely works of art, lacking in necessary details such as a drive train and chain.

Eine Spielerei aus Schrift und Design, ein Gestaltungsprojekt ohne Verwirklichungsanspruch. Die Write-a-Bike-Idee des Schweizer Designers und Schriftgestalters Juri Zaech, der in Paris lebt, besticht durch ihre Leichtigkeit und organische Verbindung von Schrift und Hardware, sprich: dem Rahmen des Fahrrads. Auf den ersten Blick scheinen die Entwürfe lebendig und dreidimensional. Erst beim näheren Hinsehen entpuppen sich die Räder als reine Kunstwerke, denen reale Kleinigkeiten wie ein Antrieb und eine Kette fehlen.

Un jeu d'écriture et de design, un projet de conception sans contrainte de faisabilité. L'idée Write a Bike, du créateur de typographies et designer suisse Juri Zaech installé à Paris, saisit par sa légèreté et la relation organique qui unit l'écriture au matériau dans le cadre de la bicyclette. Au premier regard, les esquisses semblent tridimensionnelles, voire vivantes. Il faut observer attentivement les vélos pour se rendre compte qu'il s'agit purement et simplement d'œuvres d'art auxquelles il manque un pédalier et une chaîne.

COMES WITH CURVES

CYCLONE VANHULSTEIJN, VANHULSTEIJN

A one-off becomes a bike company. Herman van Hulsteijn built an unusual bike for personal use, and the powerful response to his creation led to a career change. The Dutch interior designer now sells a curvy hand-built, stainless-steel frame with custom fittings. The basic versions comes as a single-speed or a 3-11 hub with rimbrakes, also a racing version is available. The Cyclone's shape polarizes and astonishes traditionalists who can't accept anything without a diamond frame.

Vom Einzelexemplar zur Bike-Company. Herman van Hulsteijn baute ein ungewöhnliches Rad zum persönlichen Gebrauch, die starke Resonanz darauf führte zum Berufswechsel. Der niederländische Interior-Designer verkauft nun seine kurvigen Edelstahlrahmen, handgemacht und mit individueller Ausstattung. Die Grundversionen kommen als Singlespeed oder mit 3- und 11-Gang-Naben-schaltung mit Trommelbremsen, auch eine Rennversion ist erhältlich. Die Form des Cyclone polarisiert und verwundert Traditionalisten, die den Diamantrahmen als unumstößlich ansehen.

De l'exemplaire unique à la production commerciale. Herman van Hulsteijn a conçu ce vélo non conventionnel pour son utilisation personnelle, mais sa forte notoriété l'a poussé à revoir sa carrière professionnelle. L'architecte d'intérieur néerlandais vend désormais ses cadres d'acier aux courbes caractéristiques réalisés artisanalement et les pare d'un équipement personnalisé. Les versions de base viennent avec trois ou onze vitesses intégrées et des freins à tambour. Il y a aussi une version competitive. La forme du Cyclone est saisissante et déconcerte les puristes attachés aux cadres en losange.

Country: Netherlands · Year: 2010 · Weight: 10 kg · Frame: Stainless steel · Gears: 1–14, internal hub system or derailleur · Tyres: 28" · Brakes: Rim brakes, coaster brake

A RACER IN DISGUISE

SPEED, MOULTON

It's the classic wolf in sheep's clothing. The Moulton Speed looks like the familiar British small-wheeled bike but it's actually a high-performance racing machine. Originally designed for the prestigious Race Across America (RAAM), this latest version of the Speed bike has the typical tubular space frame design constructed from the finest stainless-steel tubing from Columbus and Reynolds. Even the seat post and stem are composed of Reynolds 953 stainless-steel alloy from England. The Moulton Speed's geometry is designed for an extremely athletic riding position.

Der klassische Wolf im Schafspelz. Das Moulton Speed sieht aus wie das bekannte britische Klapprad, ist aber ein Rennrad mit extra kleinen Rädern für höchste Leistung. Ursprünglich für das prestigeträchtige Race Across America (RAAM) entworfen, wird die neueste Version des Speed in feinstem Edelstahl von Columbus und Reynolds mit dem typischen Gitterrahmen des Space-Designs gefertigt. Auch Sattelstütze und Vorbau bestehen aus der englischen Edelstahllegierung Reynolds 953. Die Geometrie des Moulton Speed ist auf eine extrem sportliche Sitzposition ausgelegt.

Le cas typique du loup déguisé en agneau. Sous les traits du traditionnel vélo pliant britannique se cache en réalité un vélo de course des plus performants. Originalement conçu pour la prestigieuse course Race Across America (RAAM), le Moulton Speed présente une géométrie extrêmement sportive. Si elle reprend la typique structure treillis de la conception spatiale, la dernière version du Speed fait appel, pour le cadre, la tige de selle et la potence, aux tubes d'acier Reynolds 953, l'exceptionnel alliage anglais d'acier inoxydable.

Country: United Kingdom · Year: 2011 · Weight: 9 kg · Frame: Aerospace stainless steel
Gears: Campagnolo Super Record 22, with special Moulton 10-28t sprockets
Tyres: 20" · Brakes: Campagnolo Super Record

LITTLE ITALY

VELOCINO, ABICI

The charming Velocino is based on an Italian bike design from the 30's. The unusual frame design and extremely small front wheel result in compact dimensions, making it perfect for carrying or for storing in small apartments. The goal of the Abici factory in Lombard is to bring back historic bike designs. Once upon a time, the Velocino concept failed to achieve recognition. Today its unusual design fascinates, and is perfectly in line with growing demands for urban mobility.

Das charmante Velocino greift ein italienisches Rad-Design aus den 30er Jahren auf. Die ungewöhnliche Rahmengestaltung und das extrem kleine Vorderrad erzeugen kompakte Abmessungen, perfekt, um das Rädchen zu tragen oder in kleinen Wohnungen zu verstauen. Die lombardische Manufaktur Abici hat es sich zum Ziel gesetzt, historische Rad-Konstruktionen wiederzubeleben. Das Konzept des Velocino setzte sich einst nicht durch. Heute bezaubert es durch die ungewöhnliche Gestaltung und entspricht dem gewachsenen Wunsch nach urbaner Mobilität.

Ce mignon Velocino reprend le design d'un vélo italien des années 30. La structure inhabituelle du cadre et la toute petite roue avant se traduisent par des mensurations compactes, idéales pour transporter le vélo ou pour le loger dans un petit studio. L'entreprise lombarde Abici s'est fixé pour objectif de faire revivre les vélos historiques. Autrefois, le concept du Velocino n'avait pas réussi à s'imposer. Aujourd'hui, on tombe sous le charme de sa structure originale qui correspond parfaitement aux besoins croissants de mobilité en ville.

Country: Italy · Year: 2010 · Weight: 10 kg · Frame: Steel · Gears: Single speed · Tyres: 12.5" (front); 28" (rear) · Brakes: Back pedal brakes

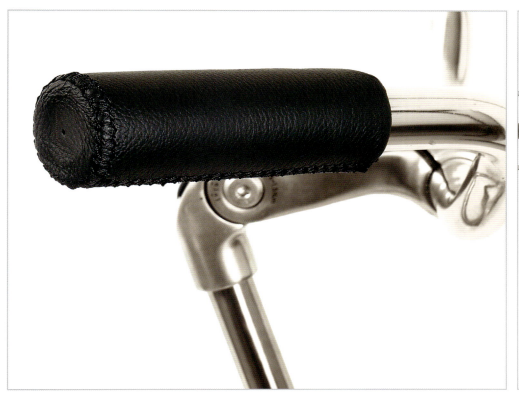

BORN TO BE MILD

VELORBIS LEIKIER, VELORBIS

Denmark meets Easy Rider. Two Danish heavyweights are responsible for the Leikier, whose design is based on chopper motorcycles from the 50's. Designer and metalsmith Lars Leikier created this limited-edition bike with its amazingly practical design for Velorbis. Its hub dynamo, Nexus 7-speed hub, and high load capacity make the Velorbis Leikier a pleasant ride and a real eye-catcher when parked in front of the supermarket—provided collectors ever allow it outside their studio apartments.

Danmark goes Easy Rider. Zwei dänische Größen stehen hinter diesem Rad, dessen Entwurf an Motorrad-Chopper der Fünfziger angelehnt ist. Der Designer und Kunstschmied Lars Leikier entwarf für Velorbis dieses limitierte Design-Bike, das erstaunlich praktisch ausgelegt ist: Nabendynamo, 7-Gang-Nexus-Schaltung und hohe Zuladung machen das Velorbis Leikier angenehm fahrbar und vor jedem Supermarkt zum absoluten Hingucker. Falls das Rad je die Atelierwohnungen der Sammler verlassen sollte.

Easy Rider à la mode danoise. Deux pointures du design danois sont à l'origine de ce vélo, dont la conception s'inspire des choppers des années 50. Le designer et ferronnier d'art Lars Leikier a créé pour Velorbis ce vélo en série limitée, qui surprend aussi par son équipement: dynamo-moyeu et moyeu arrière Nexus 7 vitesses agrémentent le plaisir de conduite. Garé devant un supermarché, il devient l'attraction absolue ... À supposer que le vélo quitte l'appartement ou l'atelier de son collectionneur.

Country: Denmark · Year: 2010 · Weight: 18 kg · Frame: Aluminium · Gears: Shimano Nexus 7 Speed · Tyres: 26"
Brakes: Drum brakes (front); roller brakes (rear)

THE REAL SHOW-OFF

DCM CHOPPER SKURUS, DEGINDER CYCLE

"Anything to get attention" could be the motton of this manufacturer! The Deginder Cycle factory in Berlin-Charlottenburg manufactures one-of-a-kind design pieces on two wheels. Whether crocodile or ostrich leather, chrome components or longhorn handlebars like those on the DCM Chopper, and customers' wishes and imaginations know no bounds. Company head Dirk deGünther pulled out all the stops for this extreme rebuild and equipped the "Skurus" with a six inch-wide fat-boy rear tire.

Auffallen um jeden Preis. Die Deginder Cycle Manufactur fertigt in Berlin-Charlottenburg einzelne individuelle Designstücke auf zwei Rädern. Fantasie und Kundenwünschen sind keine Grenzen gesetzt. Egal ob Kroko- oder Straußenleder, Chromkomponenten oder wie beim DCM Chopper ein superbreiter Lenker aus Horn. Firmenchef Dirk deGünther zog beim Extrem-Umbau alle Register und stellte den „Skurus" auf einen Fat-Boy-Hinterreifen mit sechs Zoll Breite.

Tout pour le show. L'entreprise Deginder Cycle réalise dans le quartier de Berlin-Charlottenburg des objets design à deux roues totalement sur mesure. L'imagination et les désirs des clients ne connaissent aucune limite, car le patron Dirk deGünther met tout en œuvre pour ces préparations spéciales: cuir d'autruche ou de crocodile, chromes rutilants ou encore guidon extra large fait de deux cornes comme pour ce chopper DCM. De plus, le «Skurus» est équipé d'un pneu arrière Fat-boy d'une largeur de six pouces.

Country: Germany · Year: 2011 · Weight: 32 kg · Frame: Alloy
Tyres: 24 x 3.5" (front); 25 x 6.0" (rear) · Brakes: BACK BREAK-DISC 240 mm

A RIDE ON JEWELLERY

LUXURY GOLD, MONTANTE CICLI

Twenty-four-carat gold leaf and 11,000 Swarovski crystals adorn the Montante Luxury Gold. The fenders are steam-bent wood. The sparkling crystals are luminescent and gold. The python leather on the handlebars, seat, and around the lock provide additional visual accents. Calogero Montante established his bike workshop in his tiny native village of Serradifalco in Sicily. There are only ten Luxury Gold bikes in existence, available at a collector's price of over 30,000 euros.

24 Karat und 11 000 Swarovski-Kristalle schmücken das Montante Luxury Gold. Die Schutzbleche sind aus dampfgeformtem Holz, die Kristalle funkeln in Gold, die Python-Schlangenhaut auf Lenker, Sattel und um das Schloss setzt weitere optische Akzente. Calogero Montante gründete seine Radmanufaktur in seinem kleinen sizilianischen Geburtsort Serradifalco. Lediglich zehn der Luxury-Gold-Exemplare gibt es weltweit zu einem Liebhaberpreis von über 30 000 Euro.

Le Montante Luxury Gold est rehaussé d'or 24 carats et de 11 000 cristaux Swarovski qui scintillent sur la peinture aurora boreale et or. Le bois des garde-boues, courbé en étuve, ainsi que la peau de python qui recouvre le guidon, la selle et le cadenas, soulignent l'exclusivité de cette monture. Calogero Montante a fondé son atelier de cycles dans son village sicilien natal: Serradifalco. Les dix exemplaires du Luxury Gold qui existent dans le monde sont réservés aux amateurs prêts à débourser plus de 30 000 euros.

Country: Italy · Year: 2009 · Frame: Chromoly steel, micro fuse conjunctions · Gears: Fixed gear / freewheel · Tyres: 700 x 35C
Brakes: Disc brake with golden edition sheath; counter-pedal rear brake

THE FAST ONE

MASERATI 8CTF, MONTANTE CICLI

A traditional Sicilian bicycle company builds for Italy's finest sportscar manufacturer. While disc brakes with finely crafted fork dropouts and high-profile rims indicate speed and cutting-edge, the Columbus steel frame, short drop-down handlebars from a track bike, and the forged crank arms say retro. The bordeaux paint matches the original color of the legendary Maserati 8CTF racecar. A limited run of only 200 bikes has been issued to commemorate the 200 laps completed by Wilbur Shaw in an 8CTF when he won the Indianapolis 500 in 1940.

Ein sizilianischer Traditions-Radhersteller baut für Italiens feinste Sportwagenmanufaktur. Während die Scheibenbremse mit dem fein gearbeiteten Gabelausfallende und Hochprofil-Felgen Speed und Aktualität signalisieren, stehen der Columbus-Stahlrahmen, der kurze Drop-down-Lenker von Trackbikes und die geschmiedeten Kurbeln für Retro. Die bordeauxrote Lackierung entspricht der Original-Farbgebung des legendären Rennwagens Maserati 8CTF. Das Bike gibt es lediglich in 200 Exemplaren, in Erinnerung an die 200 Runden, die Wilbur Shaw 1940 bei seinem Sieg in Indianapolis mit einem 8CTF absolvierte.

Un fabricant sicilien de vélos de tradition se met au service de la plus exclusive usine de voitures de sport d'Italie. Alors que les freins à disques, l'usinage de l'extrémité de la fourche et le profil haut des jantes témoignent d'une technique moderne, le cadre Columbus en acier, le cintre de pistard et les manivelles soulignent une esthétique rétro. La livrée bordeaux rend hommage à la robe originale d'une voiture légendaire: la Maserati 8CTF. Le vélo a été produit à 200 exemplaires, pour commémorer les 200 tours réalisés par la 8CTF de Wilbur Shaw lors de sa victoire en 1940 à Indianapolis.

Country: Italy · Year: 2010 · Frame: Steel with special edition Columbus tubing · Gears: Fixed gear / freewheel · Brakes: Disc brake with mechanical action clamp; special cover in CNC aluminium and 140 mm diameter „margherita" disc

SHINING BEAUTY

DOWNLOW LOWRIDER, SWAROVSKI LOWRIDER, BEN WILSON

British designer Ben Wilson's first lowrider, the Downlow was inspired by the California scene. "Bicycle Ben" is fascinated by bikes and skateboards. All his designs and drawings revolve around urban mobility and street style. The original Downlow was adorned with over 100,000 Swarovski crystals. Wilson, who studied at the Royal College of Art, says the crystals gave his spectacular Swarovski lowrider " a snakeskin look."

Inspiriert von der kalifornischen Szene, baute der britische Designer Ben Wilson seinen ersten Lowrider, den Downlow. „Bicycle Ben" faszinieren Bikes und Skateboards. Seine Designs und Entwürfe drehen sich immer wieder um urbane Mobilität und Street Style. Das Urmodell des Downlow veredelte er mit weit über 100.000 Swarovski-Kristallen. „Durch sie erhält der Lowrider eine Haut wie ein Reptil", so Ben Wilson, der am Royal College of Art studierte, über sein aufsehenerregendes Swarovski-Bike.

Inspiré par l'école californienne, le designer britannique Ben Wilson a créé son premier custom lowrider: le Downlow. «Bicycle Ben» est un passionné de cycles et de skateboards. Ses créations et ses concepts tournent toujours autour de la mobilité urbaine et du street style. Le modèle original du Downlow était rehaussé de plus de 100.000 cristaux Swarovski. «Ils donnent au lowrider une peau de reptile», avait déclaré Ben Wilson, l'ancien étudiant du Royal College of Art, à propos de son étincelant vélo Swarovski.

Country: United Kingdom · Year: 2005 · Weight: 35 kg · Frame: Steel · Gears: single · Tyres: 20" · Brakes: Rear coaster

GOLDEN EXTRAVAGANZA

GOLDEN BIKES, AURUMANIA

Aurumania sees itself as the legitimate successor to King Midas. On the midnight-black CPH Street Night Bike, only the spokes are plated with 24-karat gold. But on the Gold Bike Crystal Edition, every component and every square millimeter is gold-plated, and the frame is further adorned with 600 Swarovski crystals. At 80,000 euros, it is hands down the world's most expensive bike. "Our intention wasn't to design a utilitarian object but to create a work of art for people to enjoy," says Bo Franch-Mærkedahl, founder of the Danish design company.

Aurumania nennen sich die legitimen Nachfolger von König Midas. Sind beim nachtschwarzen CPH Street Night Bike nur die Speichen mit 24-karätigem Gold beschichtet, wurden bei der Gold Bike Crystal Edition jedes Teil und jeder Quadratmillimeter mit Gold überzogen und der Rahmen zusätzlich mit 600 Swarovski-Steinen verziert. Mit 80.000 Euro ist es definitiv das teuerste Rad der Welt. „Wir wollten keine Gebrauchsgegenstände schaffen, sondern ein Stück Kunst, an dem sich Menschen erfreuen können", so Bo Franch-Mærkedahl, Gründer der dänischen Designfirma.

Aurumania peut être considérée comme la descendante spirituelle du roi Midas. Si dans le cas du CPH Street Night Bike, qui se présente dans une livrée noire, seuls les rayons sont plaqués d'or 24 carats, chaque élément, chaque millimètre carré du Gold Bike Crystal Edition est recouvert d'or. De plus, le cadre est rehaussé de 600 cristaux Swarovski. Son tarif de 80 000 euros en fait certainement le vélo le plus cher au monde. «Nous ne voulions pas créer un objet d'utilisation courante, mais une œuvre d'art qui suscite le plaisir», explique Bo Franch-Mærkedahl, fondateur de la société de design danoise.

Country: Denmark · Year: 2009 · Weight: 9 kg · Frame: Steel · Gears: Fixed / single speed Tyres: 26" · Brakes: Fixed

CREATIVE BIKE STORAGE

STAND UP, GET UP

BRANCHLINE, QUARTERRE

The London design studio, Quarterre, unite furniture and interior design with seeking to support everyday life on two wheels. Using their expertise in automotive design, the four Brits seek to create functional, efficient and stylish solutions. For smaller spaces Branchline can be inverted. The hand-crafted adjustable arms have leather detailing to protect the bike frame.

Das Londoner Designstudio Quarterre schlägt die Brücke zwischen Möbelbau, Interior Design und Zubehör für den praktischen Fahrrad-Alltag. Dank ihrer Erfahrung in der Automobilbranche suchen die Briten nach funktionellen, effizienten und stilsicheren Lösungen. Je nach Untergrund fixiert sich das Branchline von selbst durch die abgespreizten Standbeine. Die handgearbeiteten verstellbaren Arme besitzen Leder-Inserts, um den Rahmen zu schonen.

Le studio londonien de design Quarterre, qui recherche des solutions fonctionnelles, efficaces et stylées à partir de travaux dans le secteur style automobile, a établi un pont entre mobilier et décoration intérieure pour répondre aux besoins quotidiens des cyclistes. Le Branchline dispoe de bras adaptables faits à la main et revêtus de cuir pour ne pas abîmer les cadres. Il peut même être retourné pour économiser encore plus d'espace.

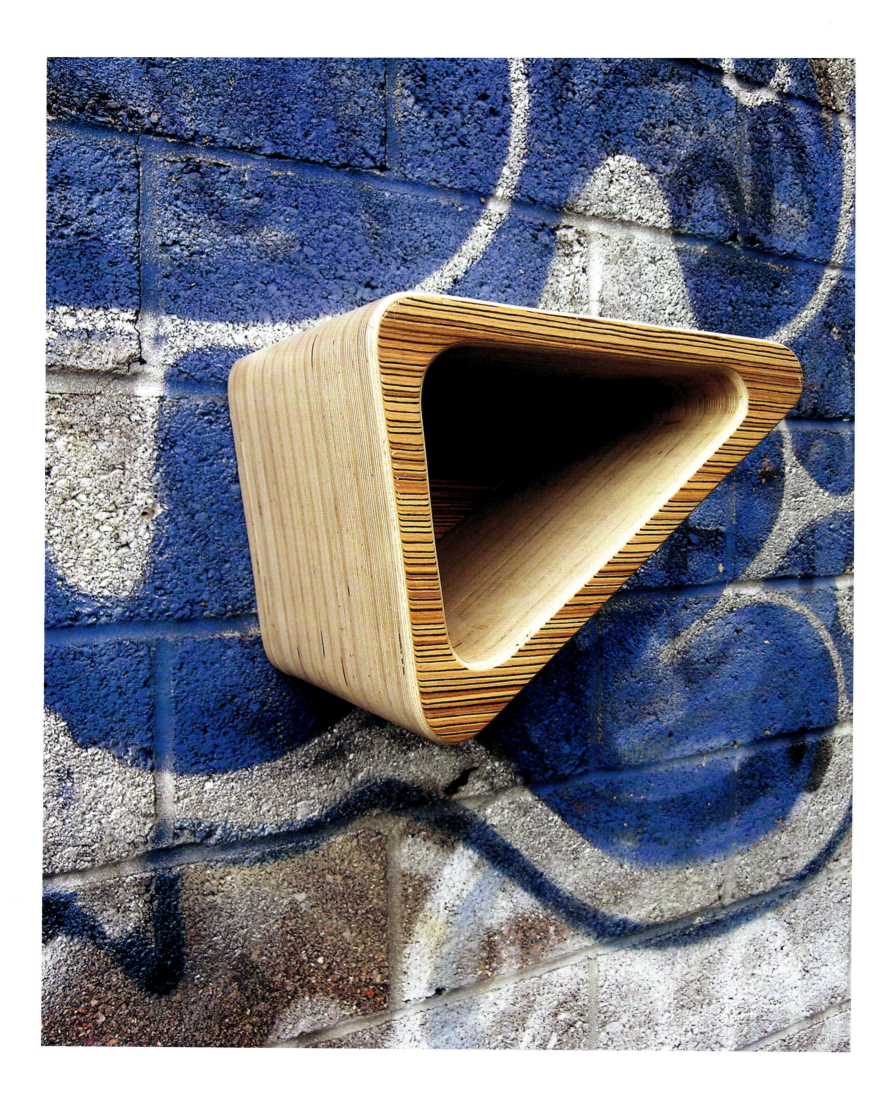

WOODEN TRIANGLE

BEDFORD AVE BIKE RACK, 718 MADE IN BROOKLYN

Simple, streamlined, compact—and because they're made to order, every bike rack produced by the Bedford Ave company in Brooklyn is a one-of-a-kind. This is the only way to guarantee that a particular frame will fit. Jeff Mayer, a former professional BMX rider, builds the Bike Rack out of birch plywood and covers it with a veneer. Of course, you can also choose your own color and paint.

Simpel, klar, reduziert. Jede Fahrradhalterung der Firma Bedford Ave in Brooklyn ist ein Einzelstück, denn es wird nach den Maßen des Bestellers angefertigt. Nur so ist gewährleistet, dass es in den jeweiligen Rahmen passt. Jeff Mayer, ein ehemaliger BMX-Profifahrer, baut das Bike Rack aus Birken-Schichtholz und versieht es mit einem Furnier. Natürlich kann man auch Farbe und Lackierung individuell wählen.

Simple, clair et réduit au minimum. Chaque porte-vélo de la société Bedford Ave de Brooklyn est une pièce unique. En effet, il est réalisé selon les mesures fournies par le client. C'est l'assurance d'un produit parfaitement adapté au cadre du vélo de chacun. Jeff Mayer, ancien cycliste professionnel sur BMX, conçoit son Bike Rack en contreplaqué de bouleau décoré d'une feuille de placage. Bien sûr, la couleur et la finition sont personnalisables.

MORE THAN JUST STRAIGHT LINES

PEDAL POD, TAMASINE OSHER DESIGN

British designer Tamasine Osher, who also studied architecture, is inspired by combining unexpected elements. The Pedal Pod, made of fine, solid walnut, is distinctive for its simplicity and straight lines. It's a piece of furniture whose form pleases even when it's not actively fulfilling its function. It also offers the practical option of storing bike accessories near the bike.

Organische Formen und Materialien in neue Zusammenhänge zu setzen, das reizt die britische Designerin Tamasine Osher, die Architektur studierte. Das Pedal Pod aus feinem, solidem Walnussholz besticht durch seine Einfachheit und Geradlinigkeit. Ein Möbelstück, das auch ohne seine Funktion als Objekt nicht störend wirkt. Praktisch: die Möglichkeit, viel Radzubehör nahe am Bike aufzubewahren.

La designer britannique et ancienne étudiante architecte Tamasine Osher aime replacer les formes organiques et les matériaux dans de nouveaux contextes. Le Pedal Pod, qui allie la robustesse et la finesse du noyer, est remarquable par la simplicité et la rectitude de ses lignes. D'ailleurs, même s'il venait à perdre son utilité, ce meuble se suffirait à lui-même en tant qu'objet de déco. Pratique: la possibilité de ranger de nombreux accessoires à côté du vélo.

AS NICE AS PRACTICAL

THE BIKE SHELF, KNIFE & SAW

Chris Brigham, the inventor of The Bike Shelf, was creating out of necessity. He wanted a suspension device so he wouldn't have to lean his bike against the wall. At the same time, he didn't want a solution that would be suitable only for a garage or basement. His approach is extremely discreet as well as elegant and simple. The Bike Shelf is handmade in the U.S. out of hickory or walnut.

Chris Brigham, der Erfinder von The Bike Shelf, handelte aus Eigenbedarf. Er wollte eine Aufhängung, um sein Rad nicht an die Wand lehnen zu müssen. Aber er wollte auch keine Lösung, die man nur in einer Garage oder im Keller benutzen konnte. Sein Ansatz ist wunderbar unaufdringlich, dabei elegant und klar. The Bike Shelf wird in den USA von Hand hergestellt, die verwendeten Materialien sind Walnuss oder Hickory.

Chris Brigham a inventé The Bike Shelf pour répondre à ses propres besoins. Il voulait un système de suspension pour éviter d'appuyer son vélo contre le mur. Mais il voulait aussi éviter une installation réservée au garage ou à la cave. Le résultat est une merveille de discrétion, un modèle d'élégance et de clarté. The Bike Shelf est réalisé à la main aux États-Unis en bois de hickory ou de noyer.

SIMPLY INGENIOUS

CYCLOC, ANDREW LANG

Bike-obsessed industrial designer Andrew Lang came up with the concept for the ingeniously simple and compact Cycloc storage system while fiddling with a pen between his fingers. Next he made a sketch model to serve the same purpose and attached this to the wall, the development process was underway. The plastic Cycloc moulding can hold most bikes horizontally, vertically, or at any angle, by using the bike's natural weight bias around the seat post or frame tube. There is room to store a helmet on top and accessories inside the Cycloc. Additionally, two holes make it possible to lock the bike directly onto the Cycloc using a conventional bicycle lock.

Die Idee zum genial einfachen und reduzierten Haltesystem Cycloc kam dem radverrückten Industriedesigner Andrew Lang, als er mit einem Bleistift zwischen seinen Fingern spielte. Der nächste Schritt war ein Plastikbecher, den er an die Wand klebte, und so begann der Design-Prozess. Die Kunststofftrommel verankert waagerecht, schräg oder senkrecht einfach durch die Spannung eines Rahmenrohrs oder der Sattelstütze jedes Rad. Im Inneren und auf dem Cycloc bleibt Ablageplatz für Helm und Zubehör. Durch die zwei Bohrungen kann man das Bike auch direkt am Cycloc mit einem handelsüblichen Schloss sichern.

Andrew Lang, à la fois designer industriel et mordu de vélo, eut l'idée de ce génial système de fixation simple et compact alors qu'il jouait avec un crayon entre ses doigts. Dans un deuxième temps, il fixa un gobelet en plastique sur le mur. Le Cycloc était né. Un cylindre de plastique maintient le vélo en position horizontale, verticale ou oblique par une simple tension exercée sur la tige de selle ou la barre horizontale. L'intérieur et le dessus du Cycloc offrent un espace de rangement pour le casque et autres accessoires. Deux trous permettent le passage d'un antivol tout à fait classique.

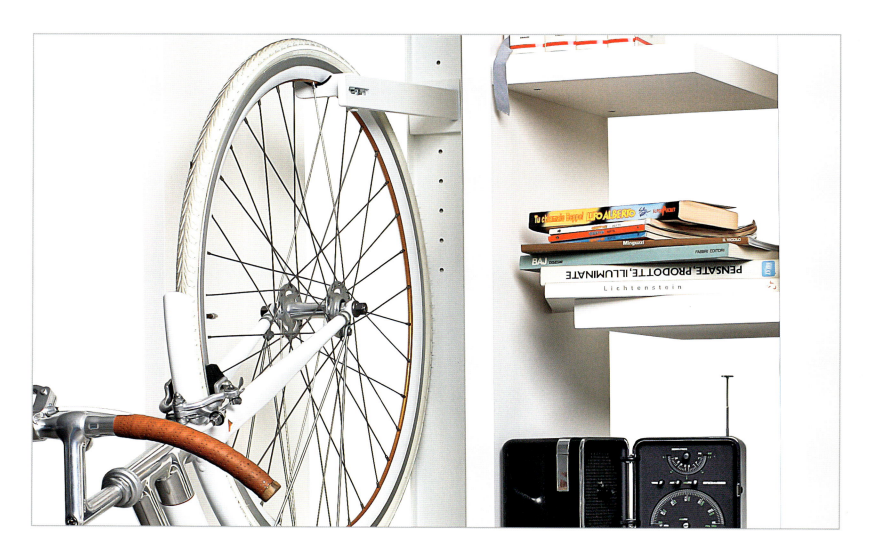

GET HOOKED

BOOKBIKE, BYOGRAFIA

Now it's possible to display your bicycle as an interior design object alongside books and CDs. These shelves—created by Italian Designer Ugo Fava of the BYografia studio—have an integrated, adjustable hook that holds the bike while also providing storage space for bike accessories, etc. Bookbike is a stylistic success and offers a groundbreaking combination of practical storage and aesthetic presentation.

Das Fahrrad als Wohnobjekt neben Büchern und CDs. Im Regal des italienischen Designers Ugo Fava von BYografia nimmt ein verstellbarer integrierter Haken das Bike in den Griff. Daneben bleibt Stauraum für Bike-Utensilien oder anderes. Stilistisch gelungen und eine neue Kombination aus praktikabler Ordnung und ästhetischer Präsentation.

Le vélo en tant qu'objet de déco au milieu des livres et des disques. Sur l'étagère du designer italien Ugo Fava de BYografia, un crochet intégré et adaptable maintient le vélo tout en laissant assez de place pour ranger des accessoires de vélo ou toute autre chose. Une véritable réussite stylistique qui marie rangement pratique et qualité esthétique.

mama BikeRack

SEEMED LIKE THE THING TO DO

MINIMALISTIC SOLUTION

MAMA, MATT ELTON AND MATTEO BALDARELLI

The name and product are a combination of two creative minds who invented this deceptively simple bike rack. In collaboration the Italian graphic designer Matteo Baldarelli and the London furniture designer Matt Elton built this minimalistic storage element from coated stainless steel. It's extremely practical in that it allows you to store accessories like helmets and gloves next to the bike. When Mama is mounted in public spaces or outside a café, the holes allow use of a lock.

Name und Produkt sind eine Kombination aus den beiden Kreativen, die dieses einfach anmutende Bike Rack schufen. Gemeinsam entwarfen der in London lebende Möbeldesigner Matt Elton und der italienische Grafikdesigner Matteo Baldarelli diese minimale Aufbewahrungsmöglichkeit aus beschichtetem Stahl. Praktisch, dass Zubehör wie Helm und Handschuhe oder Lampen direkt beim Rad liegen können. Wird Mama an öffentlichen Plätzen oder Cafés montiert, erlauben die Bohrungen eine Sicherung.

La conception et le nom de ce porte-vélo, simple en apparence, sont le résultat de l'association de deux créateurs. Le designer de mobilier londonien Matt Elton et le graphiste italien Matteo Baldarelli ont élaboré ensemble cette solution de rangement minimaliste en acier. Pratique: l'équipement, comme le casque, les gants ou les lampes, peut être rangé à côté du vélo. Si le Mama est placé sur des espaces publics ou à côté de bars, des trous sont prévus pour l'utilisation d'un antivol.

ONE CAR LESS

CAR SHAPED BIKE RACK, CYCLEHOOP

Ten bikes can fit into the space normally reserved for one parked car. This is the message visually communicated by the Car Shaped Bike Rack. This solution, by British Designer Anthony Lau, was the winner of "Best Cycle Facility" in the London Cycling Awards and was originally commissioned by the London Festival of Architecture. It can be moved from spot to spot or permanently installed. The young inventor's London-based Cyclehoop company creates a wide variety of solutions for simple and secure bike parking in congested urban areas. The rack has now found a home in cities in Ireland, the UK, Sweden, Portugal, Finland, Germany, USA, and Canada.

Zehn Räder passen auf die Fläche, die normalerweise ein geparktes Auto einnimmt. Diese Botschaft wird vom Car Shaped Bike Rack optisch originell umgesetzt. Die Lösung des britischen Designers Anthony Lau war der Gewinner von „Best Cycle Facility" der Londoner Cycling Awards, ausgewählt vom London Festival of Architecture. Das Rack kann mobil oder fix installiert werden. Die Firma Cyclehoop des jungen Erfinders in London kreiert unterschiedlichste Lösungen, um Fahrräder sicher und einfach für den Benutzer in städtischen Ballungsräumen zu parken. Mittlerweile findet man den Fahrradständer in Städten in Irland, Großbritannien, Schweden, Portugal, Finnland, Deutschland, den USA und Kanada.

Dix bicyclettes rentrent en moyenne sur l'espace de stationnement d'une voiture. Le Car Shaped Bike Rack confirme ce ratio d'une manière visiblement originale. La solution proposée par le designer britannique Anthony Lau et remarquée lors du festival de l'architecture de Londres a remporté le prix « Best Cycle Facility » des London Cycling Awards. Ce support à vélo peut être placé temporairement ou ancré dans le sol. La société Cyclehoop du jeune créateur crée à Londres diverses solutions sûres et simples pour le stationnement des vélos en milieu urbain. Aujourd'hui, on trouve ce support à vélo en Irlande, au Royaume-Uni, en Suède, au Portugal, en Finlande, en Allemagne, aux États-Unis.

PHOTO CREDITS

Cover photo (www.alexmoulton.com) by www.alexanderkoch.com
Back cover photos: courtesy of smart, Aurumania, Ben Wilson, Velorbis

p 05 (intro) courtesy of Brompton Bicycles Ltd.

SPORT BIKES
pp 08–09 (Travelissimo) by Michael Matisse, 2009/courtesy of Hampsten Cycles
pp 10–11 (Artisan Lugged Travel Tandem) Ken Toda/courtesy of Bilenky Cycle Works
pp 12–13 (Cielo Sportif Racer) courtesy of Chris King Precision Components
pp 14–15 (Cervélo R5ca) courtesy of Cervélo
pp 16–17 (Bamboo Pro/Dragonfly Pro) courtesy of Calfee Design
pp 18–19 (Plasma Premium) by Hansueli Spitznagel (details),
        courtesy of Scott Sports AG
pp 20–21 (Pro Estrada) by Pier Maulini/courtesy of Cinelli
pp 22–23 (Oltre Super Record 11) courtesy of F.I.V. E. Bianchi S.p.A.
pp 24–25 (Nightstream) Bernd Kammerer/courtesy of
        VANDEYK Contemporary Cycles
pp 26–27 (M-Bike Carbon Racer) courtesy of BMW AG
pp 28–29 (Aero 2) courtesy of Storck Bicycle GmbH
pp 30–31 (Goomah meets Lightweight)
        by Terry O'Neil photography/courtesy of Goomah/Lightweight
pp 32–33 (Time RXRS Ulteam) by Daniel Pype/courtesy of Time
pp 34–35 (Greed 29 RC) courtesy of winoragroup
pp 36–37 (29"# Mountainbike Hook)
        by Det Göckeritz/Studio Nordbahnhof/courtesy of Punch Cycles
pp 38–39 (Jekyll) courtesy of Cannondale
pp 40–41 (R.R2 FS Worldcup) O. Wittrock,
        ADP Engineering GmbH/courtesy of Rotwild Bikes

URBAN BIKES
pp 44–45 (PUBLIC M8 Bike) courtesy of PUBLIC Bikes Inc.
pp 46–47 (Paula) by Gunter Binsack/courtesy of Retrovelo
pp 48–51 (Guv'nor) courtesy of Pashley Cycles
pp 52–53 (Finkle's Monolith) courtesy of Icarus Frames
pp 54–55 (Duomatic) courtesy of Hammarhead Industries LLC
pp 56–57 (Ristretto Doppio/Black 11) by Sebastian Jezierski/courtesy
        of Creme Bicycles
pp 58–61 (Ludwig XIV) courtesy of Schindelhauer Bikes
pp 62–65 (Alley) pp 62–63 by Robert Gebler, pp 64–65
        by Ben Wiesenfarth/all courtesy of Veloheld
pp 66–67 (Columbus MS Track Bike) by John Fabrizio/courtesy of Bishop Bikes
pp 68–69 (Berlino) by Rainer Jensen/courtesy of Pasculli/www.pasculli.de
pp 70–71 (Grass Track) by Greg Page/Page One Studio/courtesy of Townsend
pp 72–73 (Ticino 20D) by Mark Clifford/courtesy of Electra Bicycle Company
pp 74–77 (Singlespeed) courtesy of Urbike
pp 78–79 (Moscova) courtesy of Bella Ciao
pp 80–81 (Birdie) courtesy of Bobbin Bikes
pp 82–83 (No.1) by Jamie Kripke/courtesy of Paul Budnitz Bicycles LLC
pp 84–85 (Spyder GT) by Chris Wimpey, 2010/courtesy of Keith Anderson
pp 86–89 (Strida) courtesy of Strida
pp 90–91 (M6L-X) courtesy of Brompton Ltd.
pp 92–93 (GrassHopper fx) courtesy of HP Velotechnik
pp 94–95 (IF Mode folding bike) courtesy of Pacific Cycles, Inc.
pp 96–97 (Bernds Faltrad/Tandem + Box by Bernds) courtesy
        of Bernds GmbH & Co. KG

UTILITY BIKES
pp 100–101 (Light) courtesy of Christiania Bikes DK
pp 102–103 (Carryo Family) by Matthias Stief, Berlin/courtesy of Carryo
pp 104–105 (Dutch Delight) courtesy of Johnny Loco Bicycles
pp 106–107 (Taga) by Yoram Reshef Photography Studio/courtesy of Taga
pp 108–109 (umaZooma) courtesy of umaZooma
pp 110–111 (Fr8) by Henry Cutler/courtesy of WorkCycles B.V.

E-BIKES
pp 114–115 (smart ebike) courtesy of smart
pp 116–117 (Gocycle G2R) courtesy of Karbon Kinetics Ltd.
pp 118–119 (Voltitude) courtesy of Voltitude S.A.
pp 120–121 (Dover 125th Impulse) courtesy of Raleigh Univega GmbH
pp 122–123 (Shadow eBike) courtesy of Daymak
pp 124–125 (Cell City) by Sami Madi, Prinzip GmbH, Munich/courtesy
        of my-e-bike.com
pp 126–127 (ODK U500 E-Bike) courtesy of Juiced Riders Inc.
pp 128–129 (Grace Series) by Nikolaus Karlinsk/Martin Bolle
pp 130–131 (Race R001) by Martin Joppen/www.martinjoppen.de/courtesy of ebike
pp 132–133 (eSpire) courtesy of Third Element GmbH
pp 134–135 (Stealth Bomber) by Nicky Hedayat Zadeh/courtesy
        of Stealth Electric Bikes USA
pp 136–137 (Blackblock Dark Custom) courtesy of www.pg.de

ACCESSORIES
p 140   (Ilya Fridman) courtesy of Ilya Fridman
pp 141–143 (Pashely) courtesy of Pashley Cycles
p 144   (Retrovelo) by Gunter Binsack/courtesy of Retrovelo
p 145   (Donkey Products) courtesy of Donkey Creative Lab
p 146   (helt-pro) courtesy of helt-pro
p 147   (Nutcase) courtesy of Nutcase
pp 148–151 (YAKKAY) courtesy of YAKKAY
p 152   (Georgia in Dublin) by Elena Hermosa (3)
        & Des Moriarty (1)/all courtesy of Georgia in Dublin
p 153   (Brompton Bicycle Ltd.) courtesy of Brompton Bicycle Ltd.

SPECIAL & CONCEPT BIKES
pp 156–159 (DV01) by John Wennerberg/courtesy of David Qvick
pp 160–161 (B2o-vélo-bambou) by Marie Flores/courtesy of Fritsch Durisotti
pp 162–163 (Woodway) by A. Velten und A. Menke-Zumbrägel/courtesy
        of Arndt Menke
pp 164–165 (Carbonwood Bicycle) by Craig Wall/courtesy of Gary Galego
pp 166–167 (Singlespeed) courtesy of Bambooride
pp 168–169 (Vestige Bike) courtesy of Schwinn
pp 170–171 (Bespoke Collection) by Adrian Van Anz/courtesy of Derringer Cycles
pp 172–173 (Write a Bike) courtesy of Juri Zaech
pp 174–175 (Cyclone Vanhulsteijn) courtesy of Vanhulsteijn
pp 176–179 (Speed) by Paul Smith (smithpic.co.uk)/courtesy
        of The Moulton Bicycle Company
pp 180–181 (Velocino) by Studio Badini S.n.c./courtesy of Abici
pp 182–183 (Velorbis Leikier) courtesy of Velorbis
pp 184–187 (DCM Chopper Skurus, Deginder Cycle) by David Burghardt
pp 188–191 (Luxury Gold) courtesy of Montante Cicli
pp 192–195 (Maserati 8CTF) courtesy of Montante Cicli
pp 196–197 (Downlow Lowrider) courtesy of Ben Wilson
pp 198–199 (Golden Bikes) courtesy of Aurumania

CREATIVE BIKE STORAGE
pp 202–203 (Branchline) courtesy of Quarterre
pp 204–205 (Bedford Ave Bike Rack) courtesy of 718 Made in Brooklyn
pp 206–207 (Pedal Pod) courtesy of Tamasine Osher Design
pp 208–209 (The Bike Shelf) by Chris Brigham/courtesy of Knife & Saw
pp 210–211 (Cycloc) courtesy of Andrew Lang
pp 212–213 (Bookbike) courtesy of BYografia
pp 214–215 (Mama) courtesy of Matt Elton and Matteo Baldarelli
pp 216–217 (Car Shaped Bike Rack) courtesy of Cyclehoop
p 218   (veloheld.lane) by Ben Wiesenfarth/courtesy of Veloheld

IMPRINT

Edited by Thomas Rögner
Editorial Management: Christina Burns,
Anshana Arora, Verena von Holtum, Sina Milde,
Miriam Bischoff, David Burghardt, Christin Steirat
Editorial Assistance: Maria Goldverg
Copy Editor: Seamus Mullarkey, Claudia Jürgens
Creative Director: Martin Nicholas Kunz
Layout & Prepress: Christin Steirat
Photo Editor: David Burghardt
Imaging: Tridix, Berlin
English translations: Christie Tam, Romina Russo
French translations: Thomas Vitasse, Romina Russo
Expert advise: Thanks to all participating manufacturers
and Caroline Elleke of Zweirad Stadler, Germany
www.zweirad-stadler.com

Published by teNeues Publishing Group

teNeues Verlag GmbH + Co. KG
Am Selder 37,
47906 Kempen, Germany
Phone: +49 (0)2152 916 0,
Fax: +49 (0)2152 916 111
e-mail: books@teneues.de

Press department: Andrea Rehn
Phone: +49 (0)2152 916 202
e-mail: arehn@teneues.de

teNeues Digital Media GmbH
Kohlfurter Straße 41–43,
10999 Berlin, Germany
Phone: +49 (0)30 700 77 65 0

teNeues Publishing Company
7 West 18th Street, New York,
NY 10011, USA
Phone: +1 212 627 9090,
Fax: +1 212 627 9511

teNeues Publishing UK Ltd.
21 Marlowe Court, Lymer Avenue,
London SE19 1LP, UK
Phone: +44 (0)20 8670 7522,
Fax: +44-(0)20 8670 7523

teNeues France S.A.R.L.
39, rue des Billets,
18250 Henrichemont, France
Phone: +33 (0)2 4826 9348,
Fax: +33 (0)1 7072 3482

www.teneues.com

© 2012 teNeues Verlag GmbH
+ Co. KG, Kempen

ISBN: 978-3-8327-9605-1
Library of Congress Control Number:
2012932110
Printed in the Czech Republic

Bibliographic information published by
the Deutsche Nationalbibliothek.

The Deutsche Nationalbibliothek lists
this publication in the Deutsche
Nationalbibliografie; detailed
bibliographic data are available in the
Internet at http://dnb.d-nb.de.